STILL HAPPY

+ THE BOOK OF HOMER

ELIZABETH BERG

A WRITING MATTERS PUBLICATION

ISBN: 978-1-974-43880-8

Author's Website: www.elizabeth-berg.net

Book Design by Phyllis Florin

FOREWARD

Lately I have begun to think about living my life in a more purposeful way. It might be a function of my age or the times in which we live (the YIKES! years, I call them), but in either case, the result is the same: I want to be more mindful of what I'm doing, and how it makes me—and others—feel. As much as possible, I want to steer my life and my work toward the coordinates of hope and joy.

I don't want to deny the fact that there is a great deal of sorrow, injustice, pain and cruelty in the world; for one thing, such awareness is provocation to come up with ideas to make things better. But I think it's equally important to be aware that something good is always on the other end of the teeter-totter, even if you can't quite see it sometimes. Happiness sometimes marches along at the head of the parade, twirling a baton, but just as often it sneaks in under the cover of darkness.

I want always to be open to the fact that in the depths of despair, something can come along that you might never have predicted, and somehow your balance is restored. It's as if you have had a very bad day, and you turn in your driveway and it's so dark you can hardly see the mailbox. You're not sure you want to open the mailbox anyway—what could be in there? Bills and junk mail. Not this time. This time you open it, and out comes some common thing that is not common at all, which reminds you of the loveliness and wonder and worth of being here.

ii | ELIZABETH BERG

Still Happy is the second book of Facebook posts that I have published, along with my friend Phyllis Florin, who once again did the art and design and handled business aspects of this book. And she came up with the headings for the entries, again, too. (She is also a fantastic writer, who soon will have her own book published.)

Many thanks to those who asked for a second book of posts: here you go! I hope everyone will enjoy reading this book, and I would like to pass on some advice that readers of *Make Someone Happy* offered: read only one or two posts a day. It's better that way.

These posts are in random order, except for those about my dog, Homer, who left the world on June 10, 2017, on his 14th birthday. I felt it would be a good idea to put all the posts about him in one place, hence "The Book of Homer," a book within a book.

I must warn you that some of the posts about Homer are very sad, but if I haven't learned that my readers can handle and understand—and mitigate!—sorrow, then I haven't learned anything at all.

You are with me in sorrow, you are with me in joy, and many of you make the recipes I post. Thank you for that. Thank you for everything.

STILL HAPPY

A WILLING HEART

My mother was an intuitive and exuberant and highly skillful gardener. Anything she grew, grew madly. After she died, I vowed to try to learn to garden just like her. I vowed to love it like her. But you know, you can't force love. Or patience. I am an impatient gardener. If I put in a tomato plant, I go running out in my robe the next morning to see if there's anything to pick. I don't have my mother's knowledge of plants and seem disinclined to learn much about them, even though I bought a very nice book for beginning gardeners. The book has been in my kitchen for months, and has been opened once, because I mistook it for a cookbook. I don't have my mother's talent for picking out what to put in pots, I'd rather just ask someone to do it for me.

But.

This year, I vowed to do it myself.

So I just came back from the store with a bunch of plants. They were not single plants that I deliberated over to see how they'd look next to each other. They were plants that were already mixed in a pot and I thought they looked pretty nice together and so *plunk*, I took them out of their pots and put them in mine. Then I stood back to admire how they looked. I did enjoy having my hands in warm earth. I did enjoy pressing on the springy dirt to get those plants more properly embedded.

Inspired by this small effort, I went out onto the front porch and got my tacky little fountain running. And now I'm going to go and buy three more plants plus a little Buddha for the front porch because looking at a little Buddha always calms me

down. I feel like he's always saying, "Acht! Don't
worry so much, you'll get wrinkles and belly aches
and *more* gray hair plus you will be focusing on the
negative when the positive is dazzling and also
here." (My Buddha is part German.)

So I'm not exactly going to be a gardener like
my mom. But I have inhaled with my eyeballs the
deep, deep red on the geranium plant, which is
exactly what I think she would have done. (This
reminds me of a poem that a kid wrote, entitled,
Rose, Where Did You Get That Red?)

In a related story: Yesterday, I went to buy
some birdseed and when I got out of the car there
was a guy looking like he was going to ask me for
spare change. Yup. "Can you spare a dollar so I can
get something to eat at the Burger King?" The BK
was next to the pet store. So I said, "Come on, I'll
buy you something to eat." As we walked to the
BK, he told me his name was Isaiah, and that that
was in the Bible, did I know that? Yes, I said. He
told me he was from New Orleans, and that he'd
been here since Katrina. He said he'd been looking
for a job, but man, it was tough. As we waited in
line, I asked him about his efforts to find work. He
said, You need an ID to find work. And I don't
have an ID. I said, Don't you just go to the DMV
or something? And he said yes but they charge a lot
of money for an ID. I thought, I have no idea what
obstacles these people face. And if I wasn't
blushing a little, I should have been. When it was
our turn, he scanned the menu and seemed to turn
into a little kid. His eyes grew wide and his mouth
opened slightly and he asked in a near whisper,
"What can I have?" My heart broke a little and I
asked him what he would like. He scanned the

menu again. A Number 4, he said. What size drink? the woman behind the counter asked, and he very carefully said, Medium. I wanted to tell him, Get a large! but it seemed the moment was lost. Cookies? The woman behind the counter asked, and he said, Nah, they bad for your teeth. So I paid for his lunch and I told him I hoped he enjoyed it, and I went to get what I needed at the pet store.

I thought about that young man later and I felt like banging my head against the table for not sitting with him while he ate. For not offering my name after he told me his. I thought, maybe I should have taken him to the DMV, but that seemed like more than I was able or willing to do. But why? He is one of those fallen in the deep water and was reaching his arm out as I passed by. Would it have been so very hard to have helped him more than I did? Was I that busy? No, I was not. Lapsed Catholic or not, I ought to go to confession. I ought to say Bless me father, for I have sinned, my last confession was two hundred years ago and I have committed stinginess and uncaring in the face of obvious need.

But, you know, with both the gardening and with the young man, I tried. And the Buddha would say, "Acht! These things take time to learn. Make your heart willing; the rest will come."

GETTING RIGHT

Yesterday, I told Bill I needed the morning to work. I've had difficulty working lately, a neck problem, so I was all fired up about getting in my study and letting things burst forth. I sat at the keyboard, put my fingers into position, and.....
and........

I looked at the orchid on my desk. I looked at my Diane Keaton mug full of Palomino Blackwing pencils ("Half the pressure, twice the speed.") I looked out the window at the birds on the june-berry tree. I examined the dirt from the garden beneath my nails. I looked at the notes for the novel I'm writing and felt like when I raise the shade of an airplane at night, hoping for stars if not angels, and see only my blank face looking back at me.

I have stood before audiences many times and said blithely, "I don't believe in writer's block. If things aren't coming, I figure it's just time to fill up the well." I still believe that, but there was such sadness yesterday, because after such a long hiatus I really wanted to work.

I came out of my office and sat dejectedly on the steps beside the side door, where Bill was saddling up the mutts for their walk. He looked at me questioningly and I offered him my palms. "I got nothin'," I said.

He nodded. "It happens."

He took the dogs out and I got an idea. I wrote a little note to him to not run off to do the errands he was going to do and went up to take a shower.

When he came back, we loaded up the dogs into the car. Homer must now be lifted into the back of the SUV, an indignity he endures, and I'll tell you, if dogs could blush, that's what he was doing yesterday when he had to forgo his mighty leap of old for this humiliating assist. Especially after Gabby sailed past him, flying through the air with the greatest of ease, as they say. No matter. We took a long, long ride on little two-lane back roads, my favorite, with no particular destination in mind. We passed through the small towns you can still see on Route 66, passed by farmhouses and waving fields of wheat, passed by signs for eggs for sale, and many breakfast cafes on main streets, the kind that make you wish it was morning, the sun a red disc rising, and you hungry as the proverbial bear. The sky was full of clouds and I made things out of them. One was a poodle standing on his hind legs conducting an orchestra. Thin lines of swirled clouds looked like someone was making a heavenly marble cake.

Both dogs and people ended up having hamburgers for lunch and the people also had turtle sundaes. One of the people dripped hot fudge on her blouse, which was fine with her, it felt like an organic girl scout badge.

I remembered how open air brings solace, how the color green brings calm, I experienced the joy of watching little kids sitting at a restaurant table swinging their legs while they built forts out of french fries.

Last night, when I closed my eyes for sleep, the day lay on me like a fine cotton blanket. All was right: I had been far away, and now I was home, and all the little ragged edges were soothed.

This morning, Gabby lay her muzzle on the edge of my bed.

"Hey," I said.

"Hey," she said. "Can we get hamburgers again today?"

"No," I said.

Then she, being a dog, and too smart for regrets or recriminations, went out into the back yard where she got into a fine fight with another dog. Never mind that there was a fence between her and the trouble-seeking dog I like to call Cujo, it was still an exhilarating experience. She "fought," then walked away, her tail wagging, found her purple octopus toy and threw it around for herself. Gabby never needs a car ride to get herself right, but I'm glad she came with me yesterday while I did just that.

MY WISH

If a genie appeared and asked what my wish was for today, I would ask to be a fly on the wall when the candidates for President of the United States are alone and preparing for bed, especially if they take a moment to look into their own eyes in a mirror. Also, I want to see their pajamas. Then I would hope very much that I could stop being a fly, even though the idea of compound eyes holds some appeal.

FAIR MEMORIES

The Minnesota State Fair. Do you love it or hate it, or both? I love it. It is part of my family history, and here's one of my favorite memories: I was nine years old and early on a summer Saturday morning, I was sitting on the living room floor in front of the TV watching my line-up: Mighty Mouse, Fury, Sky King. I had a Pixie cut and was in love with Gene Autry. Actually, I still am, but that's another story.

I was watching TV and counting the money in my Mason jar that I had saved for the fair. My father came down the stairs and I froze. He had just returned from Korea after having been gone 18 months and so although he was deeply familiar to me, he was also a stranger. I was shy around him. He was wearing a t-shirt and his Army pants and he was barefoot. He had shaved, I could smell Old Spice. His thick hair was wetly combed back, he used to have such thick hair before he had to resort to his comb-over (which I must say was *much* more tasteful than Trump's). My Dad had a big round mole on one foot which both grossed me out and interested me. I stared at his foot because I was to shy too look at his face.

"Whatcha got there?" he asked, meaning my Mason Jar.

"Money for the fair," said I, in my tiny scared-of-my-Dad voice.

He reached into his pocket and pulled out his wallet and gave me a twenty dollar bill. TWENTY DOLLARS!!!!!!!! my brain screamed, but my tiny voice said, "Oh! That's okay."

"Take it!" he said and boy, did I.

At the fair, I went on rides. I ate caramel apples and cotton candy and a bazillion other things. I watched those magnificent horses pull the beer truck down the street. I saw Princess Kay of the Milky Way in her crown and I saw the butter head sculptures. I stood gaping at the Old Mill ride which was lascivious because people *kissed* in there. It was dark and people *kissed*, and I could hardly wait my turn to go in there and smooch. I was going to wear a white dress and a heart locket and a ribbon in my hair and Friendship Garden perfume. Maybe nylons, if I could get away with it.

I bought things at the fair that day to take home: a poster of a mare and her colt lying in a field of flowers. And my favorite: a little lantern that glowed Gatsby green.

My Dad was home. I was practically a millionaire. And the fair was there for many days and nights, and every night, there were fireworks.

Here's another memory: I remember my dad telling me that when he first took a date there, he gave her money to get in the gate, but he snuck under the fence and met up with her inside. He was poor, but he was a gentleman. As for my mom, she used to go with her large family to the fair and they couldn't afford to buy fair food. So they brought a picnic basket and my grandfather made everyone Denver sandwiches. "And oh, they were so good," my mom said. I could almost taste them. That is one reason we share memories, to give to another what we once had.

See you at the fair. I'll be the one with cheese curds stuck between my teeth and a gladness in my heart that even though so many people in my life have gone, there is that big Ferris wheel at the Minnesota State Fair, turning, turning, turning.

SOUL SHAKING

Again. This morning, I pointed to a headline in the newspaper, President Obama saying we would "not give in to fear." [This was in the wake of the Orlando shootings.]

"How many more times are we going to have to read headlines like this?" I asked. And Bill said, "As long as we are like this."

I sat staring at the headlines, at photos of people weeping in each others' arms. I was undone by text messages of people whose last typed words were, "I'm going to die. I love you all." To me, this seems like the ultimate act of generosity: to use what you believe will be your last moments to express your love to others rather than raging against your fate.

Well, I am giving in to fear. I am giving in to it in this way:

I am looking upon this latest as being scared into opening my eyes each morning remembering that life is ever-fragile and that I should not put off anything that comes from an impulse of love and caring, however vague or small it might seem. A peanut to an elephant is still feeding. I want to work harder in whatever way I can against what I think fuels this kind of violent behavior, to offer to myself and others things that provide enlightenment, joy and peace. I know this sounds like the usual platitudes. Still. It is a vow that has ratcheted up in a significant way. I feel like the water has risen to just beneath our noses. I feel we need to reach deep inside ourselves and grab our souls and shake them out in the air and the sunshine and start again.

For my part, I will try harder to be the change I want to see, and what I get now is that this needs to be a breathe-in-and-breathe-out constant. It needs to be less an idea for something to do on a random day than a way of being. As a human being with parts made by the Fly-By-Night Factory (I.M. Random, proprietor), I have no illusion that I'll succeed in the way that I want to, but it is a privilege to try. Boy, is it a privilege.

DISCOVERIES

Yesterday, Bill and I went to Chicago's Chinatown to have a look around. There is something quite wonderful about being in a place so full of things that are totally unfamiliar to you. In one store all kinds of mysterious things were kept in huge glass jars.

"What do you think *this* is?" I kept whispering to Bill, though why I felt I had to whisper I had no idea. His response each time was the same: a shrug of the shoulders and a respectful widening of the eyes. I tried to ask one of the shopkeepers about a certain kind of tea, but she didn't speak English and I don't speak her language, so we got no further than a lot of head-nodding and smiling. Still, nothing wrong with that, and I ended up buying a familiar tea, jasmine green tea, and I had some last night and it's lovely.

It was a long ride home through a lot of different neighborhoods, including Pilsen, the Mexican neighborhood, where there were so many stores with dresses that looked like Cinderella come to life, those floor-length creations with fuller-than-full skirts, in colors that astound the eye. There were stores with boots and cowboy hats, and lots of carts set up here and there selling the equivalent of snow cones. Music was blasting—lots of triumphant horns!—and there was an air of happiness and industry in the air.

Back home, we sat on the deck and had a glass of wine and the dogs lay peacefully beside us. Then we took them for a walk to the school-yard, and I had my usual fine time watching little kids play. What a lesson in creativity they are, just making things up on the spot, and what a lesson in cooperation, with everyone working together to make seem real whatever fantasy they're spinning. Little kids for president, that's what I say.

Just before dusk, when the light hangs between butterscotch and rose, I wanted to take another walk, ever hopeful that mid-block somewhere, I'd drop five pounds. Bill came along, and at the corner, I wanted to turn right to go to the center of town, and he wanted to go left to stay in the neighborhood.

"You always go the same way!" he said.

Well, first of all, not always. Secondly, I like to go the same way because it's not the same way at all. Meaning that if you look, you'll see how much has changed in only one day. In the gardens. On the street. In the trees. In the variety of citizens you pass by. "Think if you were the mayor of this town," I told Bill. "Think about what it would be like if you could greet everyone and then ask for suggestions for how to make this a better place." "They'd never elect me," he said, in his Eeyore voice, and I said, "YES they would!" in my Pollyanna voice.

I like the center of town because you see a denser population of people and dogs. In the park last night, there were two women sitting quietly on a bench on either side of a bulldog. He was sitting and staring benignly straight ahead, and it would have fit if he'd had an open book beside him and bifocals at the end of his snout. I had a fantasy that if I took the dog aside and told him he was not a human he'd say, "What do you mean?" and I'd say it again and he'd say, "Huh.

Well that's a relief. I was getting worried about paying taxes."

Here's the best part. Before sleep, I read an introduction by Jane Smiley to a collection of short stories—*Family Furnishings*—by that master of fiction, Alice Munro. She describes Munro as "a wise woman who did not start out intending to show us anything, but started out intending to discover everything." Of her intentions, Munro herself says, "What I wanted was every last thing, every layer of speech and thought, stroke of light on bark or walls, every smell, pothole, pain, crack, delusion—held still and held together—radiant, everlasting."

And I loved this, by Smiley:

"A writer of stories is a receiver of tales, gossip, anecdotes, and incidents, a person so alert, so attentive, so imaginative that any event might be made into a work of art."

You can flip to any page in a book by Munro and find any line and be charmed or galvanized or inspired or delighted or dazzled. Let's try it:

"Alfrida gave a great, approving laugh, showing her festive teeth."

I rest my case.

EAT AND BE MERRY

I just got sent some photos of a friend of mine who turned 75 and she is absolutely gorgeous. I mean seriously gorgeous. I stared and stared at the photos, and I got a little bit jealous that she looks so fine and I just keep getting fatter. Then I got kind of miserable and determined, saying Okay, I'm going on a diet, I'm going to get a better haircut, I'm going to work out, I'm not going to eat so much bread. Or potatoes. Or butter. Or cookies. Or pie. All these resolutions made me very tired and cranky. I thought about another friend of mine who used to be really thin telling me, "Oh, the hell with it. I just want to be a fat and happy grandma."

What to do? I went to get a salad for dinner but then I accidentally added a pepperoni pizza. Honestly? Not only do I not have the discipline to diet, I don't have the interest. What I want to work on is not my abdominal muscles but my spirituality and the creation of peace and happiness in my heart.

However.

I am going back to yoga. And I am going to continue to walk an hour a day because it's good for me, yes, but also because it's wonderful to see the chickens that live around the corner and all the dogs who raise their eyes up to me as I pass and all the little kids on the swings and all the moms smiling at those kids so hard it looks like their mouth might break, and all the people sitting at all the outdoor cafés, and all the fireflies that come out at dusk like little floating lanterns.

APPLE WALNUT SALAD WITH BLUE CHEESE VINAIGRETTE

This salad makes eating salad great. You do not feel deprived, but you do want more.

1/4 c. chopped walnuts
1 T. white wine vinegar
2 t. olive oil
2 t. honey
1/4 t. salt
1/8 t. pepper
2 T. really good quality blue cheese (splurge on this, it really makes a difference)
1 large head Bibb lettuce
1 or 2 Pink Lady apples

Mix the dressed in the bottom of a mixing bowl. Dump in other ingredients. Toss. Voila!

DOG AIRLINES

If you ask me, this is an idea whose time has come: Folks, do you suffer every time you leave your dog at home even more than he does? Do you feel just terrible when, before you go out the door, you pat him on the head and tell him to be a good boy and guard the house and you'll be back really soon? Is your heart breaking when you see that he doesn't even try to come along, he just lies down and sighs and rests his muzzle on his paws? Do you worry that the pet sitter will be secretly mean and not take the dog for as many walks, or as long a walk, as she promised? Because how would you know? You can't know! You will never know!

Do you think about how when you wake up in Vacation or Business Trip Hotel, there will be no dog there to greet you like you are the real sunrise? Do you even rule out vacations because your dog can't fly with you? Do you think it's just ridiculous that more dogs can't fly, especially since so many hotels now allow dogs, and some even have dog room service menus?

Well. Imagine if there was something called Dog Airlines. The logo on the airplane tail and on the napkins and so forth would be a dog hanging out of an airplane window, ears flying, tongue hanging out. It could be a mixed-breed Everydog.

Maybe a cocker spaniel mix.

The aircraft would be designed with a big cage between two airline seats and that is where your dog would ride. Right beside you. There would be a pull-up gate for the dog to enter the cage where he would lie on sheepskin or on his own blanket from home, your choice. There would also be a little gate at the top of the cage so you could put your hand in and pet him. Imagine! You're flying through the skies with your dog beside you, not hidden in a little carrying bag under the seat, but right beside you, he could even watch the movie with you! Hey! Maybe they could show dog movies like Airbud! Or footage of squirrels trying to get the birdseed!

Turbulence? You could comfort each other. Boredom? This is where Airline Fetch comes in: one dog at a time gets to chase a ball down the aisle.

I know what you might be thinking now. What about if he has to go out? No problem. At the back of the plane is the dog bathroom. It has Astroturf and a fire hydrant. You hose it off after each use or maybe it could be self cleaning. If it's a big job, same as home, into the plastic bag and then into the garbage can.

When the flight attendants came through with the beverage carts, they would also have airplane-shaped dog biscuits for you-know-who. A friend of mine suggested that the dogs' water dishes (in the cage) be porcelain, like toilet bowls, which I thought was a great idea. Another friend suggested changing the name to Canine Airways. You can see how everyone gets all excited about this idea, they all want to get on board. So to speak.

Didn't they stop offering Sky Mall magazine on airplanes? That's because it was stupid and boring. How about a magazine with stuff in there for dogs, instead? Or Bark magazine?

Here's something I should have put first: the boarding system. You do not board by groups. Dogs would get all carried away in groups, they would think it was dog park time. They would need to board in numerical order one by one, and they would be called by their name to board. This would be practical but also fun, because did you ever notice when people meet a dog on the street they almost always ask his name? So the airline personnel would be talking into their microphone saying, Fluffy? You can board now. Buster? You're up now. It would be entertaining to hear all the dogs' names and you would be less bored and impatient to get on. And wait till you hear this: you wouldn't be getting a stomach ache thinking, will my baggage fit? Am I going to have to check my luggage at the last minute and wait a thousand hours to get it? No. Because a feature of dog airlines Is that the storage bins are much bigger so no one will get an unwelcome, last minute surprise: "Sir? That bag won't fit. You're going to have to gate-check it."

Cost. The cost for a dog seat is the same as a people seat. So many people would have no problem with this. So many people would not even mind paying more for their dog seat. And incidentally, I would fly Dog Airlines even if I wasn't flying with my dog because you would be guaranteed a good seatmate.

Isn't this a good idea? If you're not sure, ask your dog.

THE HAPPY VILLAGER

This morning, I sat down with a cup of coffee and *The New York Times* and, a few minutes after reading the grim stories, began to cry. This is becoming increasingly common for me. I am sorry to admit what a wuss I am, but there you have it. Well, I put down the front page of the Times and turned to the recipe for fried chicken in the Chicago Tribune. Then, for an even higher dose of Vitamin Cheer I went outside in my robe and pajamas. In the back yard where the dew was still on the flowers and the grass was soft and damp beneath bare feet, I threw Gabby's purple octopus for her many times, and she ran around squeaking it before she brought it back to me. Everything about her said, "Ain't life grand?" She was wagging her tail in circles, always a comical and joyful sight.

When I came back in, I told Bill, "I'm afraid I'm going to have to subscribe to a new newspaper: *The Happy Villager.*"

I want to be a responsible citizen. I don't want to bury my head in the sand. I want to work hard to try to make a better world not just for our beautiful children and grandchildren but for our beautiful old people and our beautiful selves. But I am also going to take breaks as needed to go to the land of the hollyhocks beckoning with their outsized blossoms that look like crepe paper, the shrub roses growing in profusion next to the lavender. I'm going to take even more walks to regard my species doing things that are sweet and peaceful and bring no harm to anyone or anything. (Yesterday, when I took a walk to get rid of some dread and despair, there was a Golden puppy playing in the park, off his leash, wagging his tail so hard it nearly knocked him off balance. There were three people lined up on a park bench eating ice cream cones. There was a solitary philosopher lying in the grass and gazing upward. I mean, for example.)

We live in such hard times. We need to take care of ourselves so that we can take care of others. Therefore the onus is as much on us to seek out and bask in little pleasures (or big ones), to relish or become demonstrations of love and content, to celebrate nature's beauty and humanity's worth—as it is to read the newspaper and write our congress people and vote in November.

Welcome to the first edition of *The Happy Villager.*

GABBY FOR PRESIDENT

Now, more than ever: Gabby the dog for President!

Qualifications: Immeasurable loyalty. Incapable of lying. Full of love and good intentions. Comes when called. Doesn't know the meaning of the word ego. Treats everyone the same, no matter who they are or where they came from. Extra perk—budget for her wardrobe, hairstylist and make-up artist: zero.

MUSINGS

This evening I came out of the library and there was a movie showing in the adjacent park. All these people, including little kids, out on blankets on a summer night, watching a free movie. Fireflies flitting around. That was good.

I rode my bike home and I thought of a man I saw on the playground near my house teaching his maybe seven- or eight-year old son to ride a two-wheeler.

"There you go!" he said, as his son began tentatively pedaling. But his son put down his feet, stopping himself, and bawled, "I can't *do it!*"

"You can do it," his father said. "Go ahead. Start again." The boy tried again and started drifting over toward the curb. He put down his feet again and said, "*I can't do it! I'm going to go into the streeeeeeet!*"

I got home, did about an hour's worth of work and then took the dog out. I went past the playground again and saw the same boy riding around triumphantly in circles. Then his dad called him over and they did about ten high-fives in a row. I stood there, watching. I wanted to yell, "You did it! Good for you!" but I thought they'd stop celebrating and look over at me and the kid would say "Who's that?" and the father would say, "Beats me." I left them to it, but boy did I smile.

That was better.

ESSAY: SONG SUNG TRUE

Like so many others, I am living in a state of near-constant anxiety these days. Something that helps me is words, whether it's stories or essays or poems. I am offering you a little essay here, in case you too need to get lost for a little while. I hope you sail away in a little boat the whole time you're reading, and come back spiritually refreshed. Now, more than ever, let us offer to each other all that we can to nourish and comfort. (I should add that I was living alone when I wrote this.)

SONG SUNG TRUE

"You were wearing your nurse's uniform when we first met," my boyfriend from over 40 years ago, let's call him John, tells me.

"No, I wasn't," I say. "I wasn't a nurse yet."

"Oh," he says. "Well, you had some kind of uniform on."

"Waitress?" I ask.

He nods, and we both smile. "I was a waitress at the Blue Ox," I say. "It was just after I'd been the girl singer in the Blue Fox." And now we laugh out loud.

We're sitting in a breakfast café about four hours from St. Paul, where I'd been visiting my mother. John is a songwriter and musician and the consummate showman: the night before I had watched him perform with his band and I was reminded of the way he seems to win over every person seated before him. He radiates a kind of goodness, an ongoing love and appreciation for the world. He tells little stories here and there when he's performing: last night he told about taking a train trip with his daughter. He told us we should all take a trip on a train. "Just do it," he said, with a touch of what I want to say was regret, probably because he knew so many of us would do nothing of the kind. People don't often take others up on sublime suggestions. We are a wary and preoccupied and stubborn species, but here's what I know: almost every idea John has is a good one.

I had a good idea on the day I married John to himself. We were young and in a kind of love and I had gone to visit him at some town he was playing in—he had sent me the plane ticket, which I thought was unbearably glamorous. We were in his hotel room talking about the way he thought he would never be able to settle down. And yet the idea of marriage did hold some appeal for him. "You should just marry yourself," I said. He thought that was a wonderful idea.

Outside we went, and, under the big blue sky and the yellow sun and the puffy white clouds we found a nice looking tree, not too small, not too big, nice canopy of shade beneath it. We stood beneath the tree and I decreed myself a minister and I said a few things about the appropriateness and joy of this union and then I pronounced John married to himself forever and ever. John looked very happy, we repaired to the hotel room to celebrate, and then I flew back home.

He wrote to me from the different cities he played in. He sent pages that he wrote at bars while he drank beer after having set up to play that night; he wrote me letters from hotel rooms. Sometimes the letters were in crayon, just for fun.

I liked when he shared new songs with me. One night he sang me a song he had just written as I lay in the bathtub. We lit a candle and he sat with his guitar on the side of the tub and sang, and after a while I sang along.

Now, more than forty years later, here we are, just the two of us, looking at each other with great fondness but also as though we are specimens in a zoo for rare animals, with that kind of respectful curiosity.

I had thought a lot about what this moment might be like. I'd imagined him looking at me after all this time, taking a private inventory of what I'd lost and what I still had. I'd wondered whether he would see past all the years into the heart of the heart of me, which would remind him that we always met most truly in a place that transcended physical appearances, though it must be said that we did appreciate each other's physical appearances, me with my long black hair, he with his soft blonde hair that shone so under the stage lights. He had such gentle hands, and some of the things we did together we had never done before.

I'd wondered if we might have a little make-out session, for old time's sake, and I had decided that maybe it would be best if we just talked. That would be making out of another, better kind, because he was a swell talker, oh, what a talker he was, he said things that were so much fun. Here is an example, although it is not something he said directly. We had spent the night together, and he'd had to leave early. When I got up and looked in the bathroom mirror, there was a note taped to it that said: NOW YOU ARE LOOKING AT SOMEONE I REALLY CARE AT.

So yes, I had imagined all kinds of things, and they all had to do with me. But there in that breakfast place, I looked at him sitting there and I saw the then-John and the now-John kind of all mixed together and I wasn't thinking about me at all. I was thinking of something I needed to tell him; it was making my heart feel stretched, how much I wanted to say this thing, and say it right.

I leaned forward and looked into his blue eyes, still so familiar to me, and I said, "John. I want to tell you something. You know how, when you haven't seen someone for a long time, you have all these fantasies about what might happen when you do see them again, about how the other person will look to you, and how you'll look to them, about what you might say to each other, what you might do together?"

He nodded, kind of sheepishly, and I all of a sudden knew a whole lot about what he had been thinking.

"Well," I said. "I had all these thoughts around you and me. But when I heard you play last night, when I saw how much you still love music and how the audience loves you.....And when you—" I stopped then, because I was getting really teary. I took in a big bumpy breath and said, "And when you dedicated that song to me and played it....." It was the song he'd sung all those years ago, sitting at the edge of the tub.

I stopped talking, remembering. The stage lights were blue and red. He played his guitar and just one other guy sang along on the harmony, and John was looking right at me the whole time.

"I hadn't played that song for so many years," he said.

I said, "I'm sorry I'm crying."

"Oh, man, just let it out," he said. "People shouldn't stop themselves when they feel like crying. Just let it go."

I wiped at my face and said, "I just feel so.... What I feel isn't about us, it's all about you. I'm just so proud of you, that you stayed true to your first love, that you are still writing songs and performing.....And also that you are still so unalterably yourself, that you are so open to everyone, that you are just you no matter who you're talking to or what you're doing. I think you're the most honest man I know." I'd spent time with him before the show; I'd arrived at rehearsal time and watched that, and then I'd had dinner with him and the band and I'd see how he interacted with a lot of different people. And he was 100% him 100% of the time.

He offered a rueful smile. "Yeah, well, I've got a lot of the coyote in me, too." He leaned back in his chair, probably to get a better look at me through his progressive lenses. "Come and see my house," he said, though I'd told him that I had to go back to St. Paul right after breakfast. "You don't have to stay long. It's on your way."

I said okay, and I followed him down some country roads and then down a long dirt road to a cabin he built. It was neat and tidy, with a kind of Western motif. I liked the kitchen a lot. His son was there, just leaving. John has two adult children that he had with one woman, but now he is with another woman. He doesn't live with her, though. And he never married either one of those women. He was already married, to a kind of freedom he can't be without.

We sat outside on his porch swing, rocking, and I said something, and he had to move closer; his hearing is beginning to go, all those nights with the band. He'd had me sit close to him at the restaurant so he could hear, too, and apologized for it. I told him never mind, I don't hear as well as I used to, either.

We sat close together on the swing and he took my hand and we stared straight ahead into the trees that surround his place, and were quiet for a while. Then I said, "Want to know a fantasy I had about seeing you again?"

"Oh, boy, I can hear now," he said.

"Okay," I said. "I'll tell you. I thought that after the concert, you'd come back to my hotel with me. And I would turn the light low and I would ask you to lie on the bed with me and we would just lie flat with pillowcases over our faces so that we wouldn't be tempted to look at each other, we'd keep our eyes closed so that we could hear better. And we'd hold hands. And I would ask you what your very first memory was, and you'd tell me."

"What's your first memory?" he asked, and I told him it was when I was three years old and riding on my father's shoulders, which I think I only did once. I was riding on his shoulders as he was walking around outside looking for my eight-year-old sister, it was time for her to come in for supper. My father stuck his fingers in his mouth and whistled loudly, which impressed me to no end, and I wanted to do it, too. I put my fingers in my mouth and blew, but no sound came out. I tried again; nothing. So I pretended I could do it. I imitated what I thought the whistle sounded like and yelled, "*fit few!*"

John laughed. Then he said, "Okay, I'll tell you a memory, but it's from when I was nine. I don't know if you know this, but I was raised Pentecostal, where they teach that God will come to earth some day and take those who are saved up to heaven, and the rest will be left behind. So I was out riding my bike one day, and a storm came, one those storms that only comes to the prairies, really violent, all this thunder and lightning. I raced home, fast as I could. My grandmother was living with us then and she was really old, she was 70, so she never went anywhere and—"

"What are you talking about?" I said, interrupting him. "You're almost 70!"

He thought about that for a moment, then laughed. "Yeah, I am. But my grandmother didn't have a car, you know, and she really didn't ever go anywhere, she was just always there. So I came in from this big storm, black sky, trees bending down, and my grandmother wasn't there. I thought God had come and gotten all the saved ones, and I'd been left behind."

He looked at me and smiled, his head tilted in a way that made me want to hold him for a good fifteen minutes. But I just smiled back.

I stayed only a little bit longer. John told me how he had planed the logs for this cabin he had built, he told me most of trees on his land were maples, and in the Fall, such reds and golds, my God....He told me it was so peaceful and beautiful there, that if you couldn't get inspired in that place, there was just no inspiring you.

He walked me out to my car and then he all of a sudden grabbed me and embraced me, a hard, close embrace, you couldn't have fit an atom between us. He said, "Oh God, now I'm crying."

"I know," I said.

I drove back to Minneapolis and listened to his CDs the whole time and some songs I listened to over and over and over again because I liked them so much. I thought about how I had watched him on stage all those years ago when we were in our twenties and how lucky I was that I got to hear him again now when we are in our sixties. I thought of how at the restaurant he shook his head and said, "I'm just so delighted to be sitting across from you." He said it twice and both times I responded by saying softly, "Me, too." I thought about how when he embraced me and wept before I got in my car, I said into his ear, "We ain't done, yet." And he said, "I know we ain't."

So there he is, living alone, not quite able to live with another. Here I am in the same situation. I thought for a whole day about what it would be like to live with him, but the truth is there isn't a chance in the world that that can happen. Pretenders and ones left behind, we're a match made in heaven that will never be a match, and neither of us would have it any other way.

WRITING WORKSHOP

I want to express my thanks to and admiration of the women who came to my writing workshop on Saturday. It is always stunning to me what happens in these groups; it seems that every single time the participants take a long dive into themselves and emerge holding a shining truth. New-ageish as it might sound, it's true. I suppose it's alchemical, in part, because of what happens when you put together a group willing to open themselves up to strangers—strangers who, by virtue of the fact that they too have opened up, become friends. But it's more than that. It's because a group of women decided collectively to take a big risk: to have the courage to look at something that had been inside them for a long time, to admit fully to it, and then make words and story of it. I think many, if not all, of them, had a moment or two of happy surprise. I hope so. As for me, I was truly honored by what they shared. This is why I read and write; for the experience of small astonishments that add up to something much bigger.

DEPARTMENT STORES

So many Macy's department stores are closing! It's due to online shopping, of course. I guess I'm getting to that sentimental phase of life, because I'm sad about this. When I read about the closings in the paper this morning, I remembered a time when I was 21 and my salary was about 10 cents a month. I used to like to amble through Dayton's department store to look at all the lovely things which I could not have, yet in looking at them this slow way, they felt for a moment as if they were mine. (I'm reminded here of my wonderful mother-in-law who used to wander around Ethan Allan after strenuous days at work to relax and pretend this was her house, no, this was, no this was.....)

Anyway, one day at Dayton's, I spied a very beautiful and glamorous gold silk nightgown, the kind of thing I thought movie stars might wear. I asked the price. $40, which in those days might as well have been $4,000. Reader, I bought it. I put it on my charge card and took a million years to pay it off and I *still* have it and it's in great shape. (I hardly ever wore it because it was too fancy but I wanted it as a kind of sign that someday I'd be doing better than I was then.)

I love department stores. I love that there are departments: clothes, furniture, cosmetics. I love the cosmetics counter, I could watch what happens at a cosmetics counter all day. I love the tall vases of flowers here and there, the dressed up, vacant-eyed yet still snobby-looking manne- quins, the beautiful displays of china and silver. I love the stories people tell me about how on special occasions they used to go with their families to this department store or...Well. I could go on and on. (Okay, just one more thing: department store Santa Land. Huh? Huh?)

At one point on this page, I talked about turning a former Borders in our village into a department store. So fun to think about having a place I could walk to where I could buy pajamas and a purse and a bottle of perfume and a sweater for my honey. I had big plans, but they were just whimsical and, in fact, impossible. So far.

So goodbye to so many Macy's stores. I guess I'll go downtown more often to visit the one we have left.

MONEY HONEY

The other day, I took a walk and I committed a sin. I had no money. You should always carry money if you go for a walk in the summer because, just like that, you could run into a lemonade stand. And if you have no money, when the high little voice asks, "Would you like to buy some lemonade?" (which is hard to do, especially for the shy ones who occupy themselves by tightening pony tails or looking away while waiting for your response), you have to say, "I would, but I don't have any money." What a dopey response. Much better to say, "Why, yes I do. In fact, I'm so parched, I believe I'll have two!"

What I ran into the other day, though, was not a lemonade stand but a pop-up store made out of a little red wagon. Leaning against the wagon was a sign saying: TOYS, 5 cents. The store was manned by maybe a five-year-old and a three-year-old. Brothers, I assumed, they had the same big brown eyes. Neatly displayed in the wagon were a bunch of cute little toys that I guess the boys had grown tired of: a rubber elephant, some hero action figure, a racing car. (Although, the little one was playing with three other toys, probably thinking, as I do whenever I contemplate throwing something out, Wait, this is pretty cool. This could come in handy sometime. Maybe I should keep it.)

Anyway, they saw me and Gabby coming from about half a block away and they assumed the pose of professional salesmen, which is to say they straightened up and clasped their hands

before them. When I came up to them, I said,
"Oh, what nice looking toys. Have you sold any?"

"No," came the stereophonic, dejected and
totally honest answer. And then I had to make it
worse. Because—you guessed it—I had no
money. Not a cent. I said, "If I had money, I
would have bought a few, but I didn't bring any
with me." They stared at me. They weren't going
to make this easy. Naturally, I could have gone
home and gotten more money and then come
back but...I don't know. It's like stealing a first
kiss. The moment has to be right. I vowed to
myself to come back later anyway, but I didn't. I
forgot. Mea culpa.

Ah well, the summer is still kicking. I'll have
other opportunities and this time I'll be ready.

One more kid thing. Yesterday, I got my hair
cut. This always makes me tense because my
hairdresser and I have an ongoing silent argument
going about how long my hair should be. I think
to my butt. She thinks to above my ears. And so I
tell her to cut off about an inch and she cuts off
about five inches. She thinks I look better; I think
I should join the marines and let them know the
buzzcut has already been accomplished.

But. The point is that in my anxiety in the
salon chair, I always look out the window. And
yesterday I saw the most enchanting pop-up play,
I'll call it. There was a curly headed little girl, four
at the most, wearing winter boots, and a very
short lilac dress that on occasion allowed a
modest glimpse of her red underpants. She was
standing on the concrete barrier of a planter
performing something that I couldn't hear but
loved watching. She faced this plant; then, that

one. Waved her arms. Bent down, hands on knees. Turned in slow circles. Spoke with what looked like a great deal of authority. Tossed her curls. Touched the leaves of the plants with great care, as though she were imbuing them with magical powers. Maybe she was, who knows? Anyway, the whole time I got my hair cut, I got to watch a kid spin things out of thin air using only her imagination and nature. What a gift. Meanwhile, her mom pushed a stroller with her baby sister up and down the walk so that her older child could finish her project. I saw all this for free. Which only reinforces the notion that the best things in life really are free: "I got the sun in the morning and the moon at night." And I have little kids showing me the best way to live.

Okay, gotta go put my headscarf on now. Can't show my hair for a good ten years.

GOING TO THE FAIR

On Thursday, I'll head for the Minnesota State fair wearing my expand-o pants. I say this as if I don't wear expand-o pants every day.

A MOMENT

Yesterday, I walked past the ice cream store, and sitting on a stone wall outside were a grandmother and a little, little kid. I'm going to guess he was barely two. There he was with his cup of ice cream, that, due to his size, looked like a silo of ice cream. He was carefully eating, wielding the plastic spoon with some difficulty. I was thinking how sweet he was, how innocent, and still a baby, in a way. Then, just as I walked by, he straightened and said to his grandmother, "Now I'm going to tell you something I'll bet you never knew." The grandmother, a woman about my age, and I locked eyes and smiled. These moments, I'm telling you.

SEPTEMBER

I always wore my new clothes on the first day of school. Even when I was living in Texas and it was over 90 degrees, I just *had* to wear the new sweater. And new shoes. Which, after a summer of going barefoot felt like jail for toes. I was so full of resolutions on the first day of school. That was the real New Year's Day for me. But by the end of the first week, all those resolutions were circling the drain, and by the end of the second week I'd forgotten what they were.

I still long for new pencils and lined paper on September 1st and I wish, I wish, I wish they made cool lunch boxes for adults. Maybe they do. In fifth grade, I used to stare at a boy named Phil's lunchbox every day because I coveted it. It was red plaid. These days I'd just come home and Google red plaid lunchbox, then take my pick. Let it be noted that there is something kind of wonderful about long-term coveting. It certainly added interest to the geography lesson.

Happy September. Here comes the fall.

DRAMA

This is why my parents called me Sarah Bernhardt:
This morning, I decided to do something special
for my dog, Gabby. I fried her an egg for breakfast. Mixed it in with her dog food. It looked so
good, I almost ate it myself.

I put her food down. "There you GO!" I said.
She sniffed it and walked away.

Oh no, I thought. She was lethargic yesterday.
This is it. She's doomed. How ironic that five-
year-old Gabby has a deadly disease and will pass
on before Homer, who's 13.

I sat at the kitchen table and thought, be
strong, be strong. I thought, you know as well as
anyone that you can never predict what a day
might bring, that all life is fragile, that we must be
appreciative of all we can while we can, and that
we must learn to curb our expectations. You
know that all the gurus teach non-attachment (but
I cannot learn non-attachment, I kind of love
attachment). But: you must take the good, try to
handle the bad as gracefully as possible—even,
though it sounds funny to say it, as hopefully as
possible. Maybe even as gratefully as possible.

But Gabby, with her sweet nature! With her
soft fur! With the way she rests her chin on my
knee and looks up at me! Sob!!

Then something occurred to me. "Hey,
Gabs," I said. She looked up. "Want some
cheese?" I asked. Yes, she did. Also she wanted
some chicken. Also she wanted a dog biscuit.

It appears that Gabby does not like eggs.
Given that Gabby can talk (as those of you who

read this page know), I wish she'd have *said* something.

Gabby: I'm too polite. I figured you'd figure it out. Can I have some more cheese? Also, do you have any prime rib?

GRANDCHILDREN

I'm off to visit the grandchildren today. I will look out the window as the plane lands and think, *Oh boy! My granddaughter is turning nine tomorrow.*

I remember being nine really well. I remember my stupid pixie haircut and how much I liked to hang from the clothes pole (no idea why) and also I liked to stand on my head.

One time when I visited, I told my then nine-year-old grandson that I remembered being nine, and he said, "I know, you told us. You had a teacher named Miss Hamburger." "Right!" I said, all excited at the memory of the teacher all over again.

Jeez. I hope I don't start telling them things I've told them before all the time. I hope this time we can just build a tent out of sheets and then eat and read in it. As you may know, eating in a homemade tent is really fun. And I hope I can stay up late with their parents and blab. That's a long shot as my current bedtime is so early I'm embarrassed to tell you what it is. I *will* say I fall asleep on the sofa before I fall asleep in bed. As though that mitigates it. As though, technically, I'm still up.

LAWN GONE

I have had it with my lawn, and I want a divorce.

It seems the only way to keep it "healthy" is to put toxins on it, even if they are organic toxins. But I no longer want to take that risk. The other day, I walked past a guy spraying chemicals all over someone's lawn. And two driveways down, I saw a dead bird on someone else's driveway. I got all puffy and self-righteous, thinking, See? You spray that stuff and *you kill birds.* Then I thought, maybe they're not related. For all I know, the bird suffered a stroke and he was 98 years old, in bird years. But I don't think so.

I walk dreamily along when I walk the dogs, and so do not always see the flags saying that pets should be kept off lawns that have been sprayed with chemicals. But birds can't read. And apparently I can't always pay attention, since sometimes I see the warning after my dogs have walked on the lawn.

I thought I should check to see if some of these chemicals coming from trucks I see around the neighborhood really are toxic before shooting my mouth off. So I looked them up. And no surprise, they are toxic: to birds, to dogs, to bees and butterflies, I assume, and guess what else? To *people*, especially children.

So I'm done. I want to get rid of my lawn. What do you think? All garden in the front? Vinca vine? Some other ground cover? I don't mind clover, but apparently my neighbors would get mad if I put in clover because the seeds would blow over to their lawns.

MY INVISIBLE BASKET

Up at 5:30 this morning. The adult part of my brain tells me to go back to sleep. But the child part tells me to get up because this is a very exciting time of day. And so I make coffee and bring a cup out onto the porch. I sit there in my dog pajamas, ready for the show. The sky is still dark, but you can tell it's ready to lighten; it's as though it's holding its breath before the big exhale that brings day back to us. It happens so gradually, you can't quite see it happening. It's like the best magic trick. Whenever I watch the sun come up, I always think about cave people, standing outside their rock houses and watching as the sun comes up again. I always wonder if they saw it as a kind of lesson in faith. And in great beauty, too, nothing like changing light patterns to make you see things better.

I see people briskly walking dogs, and the people look all officious and the dogs are wagging their tails to beat the band. I see two joggers, and I listen to the sound of their sneakers on the pavement as though it's a free song, delivered right to my doorstep.

Yesterday I was walking the dogs when I came upon a young mother working in her garden. There was a girl of maybe eight or nine sitting on the steps, reading, and a four-year-old moving around in the erratic way of the very young: over here! No! Over there! Bend down! Look up! Run around in circles! Fall down on purpose! Anyway, both girls came up to admire Homer and Gabby, even though they had their very own Golden in their back yard. The older one pet the dogs with a look of helpless love in her eyes that can be present in girls that age who adore animals. The younger girl was Chatty Kathy, and I was beside myself with delight. I heard all kinds of things, including that she was soon to turn five. (Five fingers held up, lest I not fully understand.) I had this impulse to say to the woman, "You know, if you ever need a babysitter, I'll do it for free." I didn't say it because we live in an age of mistrust and fear. However, I did stay for quite a visit with these charming strangers, and I was better off for it.

I travel with an invisible basket, and each time I take a walk, I find invisible things to put in it and carry home. Yet another reason I feel lucky.

FANTASY HOUSE

So the house across the street is for sale, and it needs major interior work. And I keep thinking, why don't I buy it and gut it and make it into the house of my dreams? That led to this question: what *is* the house of my dreams? Given my age, it would have escalators. Given my love of food, the first floor would be kitchen. Period. Well, a little powder room and the wallpaper would be butter wrappers. Basement level? TV room with divinely comfortable chairs and sofas and a popcorn maker which I used to have but gave away because I didn't want to clean it. So, right, cancel the popcorn maker. Candy counter instead. But divinely comfortable furniture and many vintage quilts and/or furry blankets to toss over you as you watch TV and another bathroom down there wallpapered with movie posters.

Second level: bedrooms with light-blocking shades that we all lusted over in the movie *The Holiday* where Cameron Diaz and Kate Winslet change houses. Beds with divine linens and down comforters. Bookshelves galore in every room. A master bath that is the very definition of sybaritic: here an orchid, there an orchid, everywhere an orchid, orchid. Bath products that smell like heaven and are expensive as hell. But I have found a way to get them cheap. Speaking of cheap, which reminds me of cheep, the walls would have murals of birds. Oh wait, I forgot, the bedroom would have stars that come out at night on the ceiling and blue sky and clouds that come out in the day. Don't ask me how. This IS a fantasy.

Guest room has books and plants and also sybaritic bathrooms and robes that are *yours* for the taking and they are much better than those robes they make such a fuss about at fancy hotels and then tell you in that snippy way that if you want one you can purchase one for ten thousand dollars. No, I give my guests robes. And they can have fancy or vintage.

A library up there on the second floor with a big globe and a big dictionary on a big stand and lovely chairs and a card catalogue, the old kind with the slide-out drawers.

The yard? An eco-friendly place with a fish pond and many little mini willow trees and a gazillion kinds of flowers.

I have to stop. I'm getting tired. Plus I want a Five Guys hamburger, it won't go away. Must not get fries. One time I asked the guy if I could just buy four fries and he just threw them in for free and *that* is a guy who has his priorities straight. Gabby gets to come for the walk and she will get two (2) bites of burger.

Oh, these last warm days. These glorious September days, the leaves asking each other, should we turn yet? One wishes one could put these lovely fall days in a drawer for safekeeping and pull one out after too many frigid winter days.

HOWARD JOHNSON'S

Uh oh. I read this morning that the next-to-the-last Howard Johnson's diner is closing. Now there will be only one left, in New York. I'd better take a trip to New York and finally get a clam strip dinner, quick.

As an Army brat, we were always moving, and we almost always drove to our new destinations. The three of us kids would be jammed in the back, and despite auto bingo and the ever-popular silent fighting, things could get tedious. My dad was interested in "making time," and so we would drive for many hours: when we stopped at motels for the night (which I loved: those little soaps! A paper band across the toilet ensuring cleanliness fit for a queen!) I would lie down and feel like I was still moving. It was wonderful to get out of the car for meals, and I always liked Howard Johnson restaurants the best. To me, they were the height of sophistication, a New York City's 21 for the pre-adolescent. They had famous ice cream. They had orange roofs. The placemats had maps with stars for cities, and I liked to dream about going to them all. There was one item on the menu, I believe it was the most expensive thing, that I used to stare and stare at before I ordered my more modestly priced toasted cheese sandwich, and that was the aforementioned clam strip dinner. *What was that?* I wondered. What *were* clams, I mean in the context of eating? How would they taste? Someday I would grow into them, and know. I don't think I'd really like them now, except for the nostalgia involved. But I still want to try them, now that I can afford them.

Ah, well. Another thing falling to the wayside, like drive-in movies. As my friend Marianne's Italian grandmother used to say, "Whaddya gonna do, go complain a City Hall?"

DUMB NUMBERS

I was out running errands and had soon to go to my writer's group, but I wanted to get a quick dinner first. I called ahead to one of my favorite Middle Eastern restaurants and asked if they'd prepare a grape leaves combo plate for me; I'd be there in about ten minutes. When I arrived at the restaurant, a table in the corner was all set up with my order, just waiting for me to sit down and dig in. I felt like Beauty with the Beast hiding nearby. I felt like when I used to come home for lunch in high school, and my mom would have my sandwich waiting there for me. Which is to say that I felt wonderfully well cared for.

I sat eating and directly across from me was a little girl about six or seven years old wearing a white blouse with a Peter Pan collar, a navy blue pullover sweater, silver sparkly pants over which was a pink skirt with a heart pattern quilted into it, and buckle shoes. Her curly black hair was in a long braid, and wispy tendrils escaped charmingly from it. She sat with a Middle Eastern man, her father, I presume, who was trying to help her with the math problems in her workbook. From where I sat, I could see how the workbook had cute little illustrations which I suppose the authors might have thought would make an unbearable task more bearable, but it wasn't working, because the little girl would try to do a problem (the pencil huge in her hand) and then, exasperated, start to cry. Her father spoke to her in low tones, and drew stick lines on the paper tablecloth, trying to illustrate how to subtract three from seven. Then he tried to illustrate the problem by putting it in terms of a food narrative: you had seven apples, you take away three, and .....? The little girl shook her head and wept.

Now, I am not one to let anything interfere with my eating, but I had to stop eating and just watch. I was dying to help, but how? I had suffered the same kind of anguish myself as a child, and still have math anxiety. If you want to reveal an inadequacy I usually strive desperately to hide, start talking to me about how to figure percentages. Or, you know, anything else involving numbers. Anytime I take change handed back to me, it is an act of faith.

The father, it just so happened, was a chef at the little restaurant. He rose to go back into the kitchen to go to work, leaving the little girl with her math homework. She strove diligently for about thirty seconds and then began to wail, a near siren-like sound serving as a wind-up. Then she sat alone, staring straight ahead, the pencil fallen from her hand, and gave herself over to her sorrow.

The restaurant was nearly empty, there were two other men customers and me, and the girl paid no heed to any of us. She wept like the world was coming undone before her eyes and her tears fell upon her merciless workbook. At once point, her head fell on the table, her forehead banged gently down, her shoulders collapsed like a flesh umbrella, and she sobbed softly away. Her poor father, who had tried to help her—had tried joking, had tried logic, had tried a mild sternness, had tried loving reassurance—was back in the kitchen wrestling with a back-up of takeout orders that needed to be prepared.

The other customers kept eating and talking but I was distraught and so I did what I so often do: *not* mind my own business.

There is a window in the restaurant through which you can see into the kitchen. I stuck my head in there and asked if I might say something to the little girl.

"Sure," the father said, and he came out briefly to tell his daughter, "This lady wants to talk to you." The girl looked at me and began to cry harder and I felt even worse for her. Maybe she thought I was going to complain about her crying.

"That's okay," I told the father. "She doesn't have to talk to me."

But he told the girl something that must have reassured her, at least faintly, and she swallowed a sob and turned her face up to me. I moved closer to her table and knelt down on one knee so that our faces were on the same level.

"You know what?" I said. She said nothing, sniffed.

I said, "When I was a little girl, I hated math so much, I used to cry when I did my homework, too. I would put down one answer and it would be wrong and then I would put down another answer and that would be wrong, too. I would erase holes in the paper."

It all came back to me, how I would sit in my room trying to do my math homework, weeping, looking out the window at the sky turning pink, then charcoal, then black, and still I had not completed my math homework, which was not my friends playing outside and was not my Black Beauty book I was in the middle of reading, and was not the bathtub filled with warm water where I liked to practice floating and to study the little water tornado that occurred when the water went down the drain, and was not the kitchen table where I sat to eat apple crisp but instead was deadly numbers that *would not give.*

"I really hated math," I said. "*Ew.*" Now she was smiling, and if you want to have your heart broken the best of ways, say something to a crying child that makes them smile.

"It will get better," I told her. And then I told her how much I liked her skirt with the little hearts and she smiled harder.

I went back to my dinner and she went back to the kitchen to sit in a little chair just for her stationed in the very back of the kitchen, out of harm's way. When I paid my bill, I saw her legs swinging as she sat in her little chair; the rest of her was hidden from view.

I wished I could take her out for ice cream and say, "Hey, I have an idea. Let's neither of us ever do math again." But instead I went to my writer's group, and I assume the chef soon went home with his tired and frustrated little girl and put her to bed and planted a kiss on her forehead and a stuffed animal in her arms, and with that, reassured her that those dumb numbers weren't the *only* thing in the world.

ROAD RAGE

I was immersed in editing today, just buried (happily) in story. I had to break, finally, and run a few errands. I got in my car, was going to make a right onto a street where the traffic was crawling along, and the woman I was going to turn right in front of sped up, leaned on her horn and gave me the finger. Okaaaaaaay. I waited for another car-length long break and started to pull out again, and *this* woman did the same thing: sped up, leaned on her horn and gave me the finger. (I know, many of you are thinking, *I bet she didn't leave enough space*, but I swear I did, I'm paranoid about that kind of thing.) Okay, so Lady Number 2 gave me the finger, and I thought, You know what? I'm going to pull in front of you anyway, and I did. The traffic was crawling, I reiterate. Well, Lady Number 2 leaned on her horn, gave me the finger again, and started yelling; I could see her in my rearview. I felt this awful sort of collapsing inside, why such *rage?*, and I stopped my car. In part it was to collect myself. In part, I confess, it was to piss her off. And of course it did piss her off and she screeched around me so that she could be directly in front of me, going one-and-a-half miles an hour. I searched for her eyes in her rearview—what is the *matter*, I thought?—and was met with what looked like hot coals. My stomach hurt for a good half an hour. Maybe hers did, too.

A friend of mine asked the other day, in light of all the turmoil surrounding the election, "Everybody says people are so *mad*. Do you think people are mad?"

Well. Yes, I do.

So here's what I'm going to do. I'm going to continue my practice of letting people go ahead of me whenever they need to pull out, unless I am on the way to the ER with a heart attack. I hope you'll do the same. Kill 'em with kindness. That's our only chance.

COOKIES PUPPIES HUGS

Recently, Saturday Night Live had an opening bit with Emily Blunt where she turned to things *pleasant*, rather than politics. It was campy, but really fun: chocolate chip cookies were brought out to the audience, puppies, and mothers giving their daughters hugs. I found it delightful. And restorative.

"Well!" I said to Bill. "There's a change!"

When I think about my work going forward, I want it to be the same way as that opening: restorative. Life affirming. Former nurse that I am, I'm interested in making people feel better, in reminding them (and myself) of the fact that even under trying circumstances life is full of beauty and of pleasures large and small. I'm interested in the idea of us puzzling things out together, of showing how much we need each other, even if (especially if) we think we don't.

MY FIRST COOKBOOK

I'm ten years old. I live on an Army base in Texas. I am scared to death of my father, whose way of telling me it's time to get up in the morning is to appear at the threshold of my bedroom, say my name and then, "Move out!" (In case you don't know, it's an Army term meaning, "Get going," not, "Find another place to live.") It took a long time for me to understand what tenderness lay beneath my Dad's tough exterior. It took until I was about 30, I'd say. But in those growing up years, I was afraid of him all the time.

So one day I'm at the PX looking at the thing I want most in the world, which is a Junior Cook Book. I look at the pictures and imagine making the spaghetti and meatballs, the jam-stuffed muffins. Each recipe in the book starts the same way: 1. Wash your hands.

I read this direction and think, I will, I will, if only I can have you, I will wash my hands very well! I will wash my hands professionally!

So on this day, when I'm once again looking at the object of my desire, my father appears. This is deeply unsettling, like seeing your teacher in blue jeans at the grocery store when everyone knows they should only be in school wearing tweed skirts and tie blouses and cardigan sweaters with a sweater guard and glasses that have an arresting cat-eye shape.

Anyway. Here he is, my fearsome Dad.

"What are you looking at?" he asks.

I calculate quickly: might I be in trouble? But no, I don't think so.

I show him the book.

He looks at it, then says, "You want this?"

I want it so much that I cannot say I want it. The best I can do is offer a shrug while staring at the floor.

He buys it for me. I take it home and lie on my bed and read every recipe, and then I start making them.

My dad liked recipes, too. He collected them like crazy and the recipes of his that I've tried have all been terrific. He was a more adventurous cook than my mom, though I did not always have faith in him. Once, when my mom was out of town, he was in charge of cooking. I sent my mom a letter I still have that says, "Dad is making chicken tonight. He is soaking it in Wishbone dressing!!!! It STINKS, man!"

Never mind. The man collected recipes, and what will follow is one of them. It's for pumpkin bread, the best recipe I've found for it.

As of now, since the day is fine, I am leaping on my unstylish bicycle (it has so many baskets it looks like the starship Enterprise) and going to Trader Joe's to get the ingredients I need.

CRANBERRY PUMPKIN BREAD

3 3/4 c. flour
3 c. sugar
4 t. pumpkin pie spice (or make your own mix of equal amounts of cinnamon, cloves, and ginger)
2 t. baking soda
1 t. salt
4 eggs
1 15-oz can solid-pack pumpkin (I like Libby's)
1/2 cup canola oil
2 cups fresh cranberries, roughly chopped
1 cup chopped walnuts

1. Wash hands (ha ha)

2. In large bowl, combine flour, sugar, spices, baking soda and salt. In another bowl, whisk eggs, pumpkin and oil; stir into dry ingredients just until moistened. Fold in cranberries and walnuts.

3. Spoon into two greased 9x5 inch loaf pans. Bake at 350 for 70-80 minutes or until a toothpick inserted near center comes out clean.

Makes two loaves, 16 slices each.
Delicious plain, with butter, or with cream cheese.

GO CUBS!

I came out of the house tonight on the way to go to the library to hear a lecture. Down the street came one of my neighbors, carrying a paper bag.

"Hey, Elizabeth," she said, and I said, "Hey!" We exchanged a few pleasantries, and then as she walked off, she said, "Go, Cubs!"

"Are you going home to watch the game?" I asked, and she said, "You bet!"

Well, I went off to the lecture and I listened attentively and then during the Q&A something strange began happening inside me. I think it was like what the werewolf feels when his humanness gives way to his animal self. I felt a certain wild restlessness, a kind of primal urge. And then I found myself putting on my coat and walking out to come home. Why? *To watch the game.*

I never watch any sports. I just don't care. No matter what it is, football, basketball, I just don't care. And golf! Oh my God! If I ever have to have surgery again, I'll say to the anesthesiologist, "Hold off, bud, don't give me any medicine, just turn on the golf game."

But sitting in the library, I was thinking of my neighbor and her paper bag that probably had fixings for nachos or something, and I thought of how I live in a city that is intensely watching something they've been waiting for for so long, and it just seemed crazy that I didn't do my little part. So I'm going to put on my pajamas and watch the Cubs. I can hardly wait for Bill to come home so I can ask my endless questions about personal habits and characteristics of the players. And about how much umps get paid. And if people with front row seats are just used to it, and therefore not appreciative, and wouldn't it be nice if they could switch seats with the guys in last row of the stadium just for an inning or so. If Bill has any sense, he will listen to the ball game in his car, in peace.

Go, Cubs! Or whoever they are.

POTUS SPEECH

Here is my fantasy acceptance speech by the next POTUS:

My fellow Americans.

Really.

My *fellow* Americans.

I want to deliver a very short speech tonight from my heart and not from a teleprompter. All the plans I have in mind for this country will be in evidence soon enough. All my plans and ideas, my convictions, my prejudices, my peculiarities, my best side to photograph, the pets I bring to the White House, they will all be in evidence soon enough.

What I want to say tonight is one thing: Let's start over. Everyone who was passionate about their candidate was that way for a reason. Tempers flared, reason fled. Ill will grew and grew. Many, if not most, people grew depressed and distressed by the vitriol in this election; and many others—I will admit it—were angered by the fact that they did not want to vote for either candidate. Many asked themselves and each other, over and over, "Is *this* the best we can do?"

But here we are. This nation has sighed and elected me as its new President.

As your leader, I'm going to give things and I'm going to ask for things. I've already asked that we start over, that we clear the slate. We need to work hard to see the best in one other, and we need to listen to one another, just in case someone we viewed as an adversary actually has a really good idea.

As for what I'll give, I'll start with an apology. I am sorry for everything you had to endure during the course of this election. Sorry and ashamed. Believe me when I tell you it was no picnic for us candidates, either.

But it's over now. Let's take a collective deep breath and then, as the yoga teachers say, just blow it all out.

May I admit something to you? I enter this job with gratitude, pride, and joy. But I also enter it with a great deal of fear. I know many of you are afraid, too. But the good part of fear is that it wakes you up and sharpens your focus, and it tunes you in quickly to the value of whatever help you can find.

I cannot do this alone. This is not my country; it is all of ours. As such, we all need to pay attention to the task at hand, which is the creation of a nation we really can be proud of, and not because it's "Number One," but because it demonstrates that it has intelligence, compassion, heart, and soul. There is still so much here to love. Forget going to Mars. Let's put money into things that will restore faith, hope, optimism, kindness and care right here on Earth.

Whew.

I'm exhausted.

Aren't you?

Let's get some sleep. And hope that tomorrow really is a new day.

I'll see you.

I promise.

PAYING ATTENTION

Today I sat in my office looking out the window for some time. Yellow leaves were drifting sideways like rain. The rose/coral leaves of the service berry tree in my front yard are hanging on, but not for much longer, I know; and I stare at that beautiful color like I can imprint it on myself, when I know full well I can't. When I know full well, in fact, that part of the leaves' glory is the fact that they are temporary and so offer a free lesson in the art of paying attention.

I watched the leaves for a while, but not nearly long enough, because I think that in order to get maximum value from one of the common miracles of nature, you have to look long and deep. You have to look so long it's as though you leave yourself behind. And then all that there is, is leaves. Or a tree. Or ripples in water. Or the pattern of birds in flight. Or the sway of grain in a field. Or the call of a loon.

It's November, and soon the snow will be falling. I am not a fan of winter, because I hate being cold. But here's what I am a fan of: classical seasons, which reinforce the notion of life as a great cycle, ever-changing. Something is always being born. Something is always dying. Those of us in the middle of things are lucky to look in both directions and see enormous value in either direction.

And now, down to the kitchen where the overhead lights are on against the grayness of the day. I'm going to make some butternut squash soup, complete with a bit of apple thrown in for flavor. And then I'll make some molasses cookies, complete with a little pepper thrown in for the same reason. I like the little things people just throw into recipes, and their lives. It reminds me of the epigraph I used in the front of *Make Someone Happy*:

"There are books in which the footnotes or comments scrawled by some reader's hand in the margin are more interesting than the text. The world is one of those books."
-George Santayana

VICKI'S WINTER MINESTRONE SOUP

In need of some comfort food? (When are we ever *not*?) I'm so happy to share—in her words—my friend Vicki Longo's recipe for a really good soup. Vicki is the one who hosted the writing workshop in Boston, and fed us so well. And took the time to type all this out so I could just cut and paste. Thanks so much, Vicki!!!

I have used this recipe for what seems like a thousand seasons and reasons. It never lets me down. What I love most about it—well, maybe not most—but what I love a lot about it, is that you can make it a day or two ahead of time so the mess is all out of the way before you serve it. Actually, I recommend you make it in advance as it gives all the ingredients a chance to get to know one another and when they get friendly like that they taste better.

Olive oil for the pan

1 large onion, finely chopped

2-3 celery stalks, finely chopped

1 lb. carrots, finely chopped

1/2 t. each: dried basil, rosemary, oregano, and thyme

1/4 c. pearl barley (unless you are making it for gluten free people)

1 can each: chickpeas (garbanzo beans), red kidney beans, cannellini beans - if you are making this for a big crowd, use two each

1 can tomato paste

1 bag of frozen chopped spinach or kale or cabbage, thawed (I usually use kale)

1 c. small pasta - shells or small elbows - or you
can leave out the pasta
8 c. chicken or vegetable stock (not broth)
Lots and lots and lots of Romano cheese

Heat the oil in the pan and add the onion,
celery, carrots and cook for about five minutes,
stirring them around.

Add the herbs and cook another five minutes
or so, until the veggies begin to soften.

Add the stock and the barley, if you are using,
and bring to a boil and then reduce heat and
cover and simmer for about 20 minutes.

Add the beans and the pasta (if you use it) and
simmer another 20 minutes or until the pasta is *al
dente*.

Add the tomato paste and mix it in well and
simmer about 10 minutes so it soaks into
everything.

Add the greens and simmer another 10
minutes so they soften and warm up.

Add a half cup or more of the grated cheese
and stir it in good. Turn off the heat and let it sit.

If you have one or two cheese rinds, they are
wonderful to add to the soup as it is cooking.
Just don't forget to remove them before serving.

Add a good crusty bread, a good bottle of red
wine, and some nice quiet music, or maybe watch
a good Italian movie—*My Cousin Vinnie* or
Moonstruck, or maybe even *The Godfather*—and
enjoy!

VICKI'S KALE SALAD

I am making Vicki's wonderful soup today, and also her fabulous Kale Salad. Also, I'm sewing. And reading. Domestics heal me. Thanks again, Vicki Longo, for your beautiful recipes and spirit. Here, again in her charming words, is Vicki's recipe for kale salad.

1 bag chopped kale (you can buy a head of kale and chop it yourself but why would you do that?)

1 package shredded carrots

3 stalks chopped celery

1 container of trail mix without chocolate pieces (it's kind of fun to buy with the chocolate pieces and then just pick them out and eat them!)

Crumbled feta cheese or goat cheese if you like - it makes the dressing creamier which is also nice

1 bottle of Brianna's blush dressing - there is a strawberry on the label because guess what? it is also good on strawberries!

Mix everything together in your biggest salad bowl the day before you want to serve it. It keeps for several days if you can keep yourself away from picking on it.

Sometimes I add frozen shelled edamame – right from the freezer – while I am mixing it.

THE DRIVE-IN

We used to go a lot when I was a kid. We had a station wagon so my Dad would put the seats down and voila, a bed for when we kids got sleepy. We put on our pajamas, and when dusk came we went to the land of gravel and gently sloping hillocks and metal speakers that affixed to the rolled-down windows (which allowed the mosquitoes in, but one had then to, and must now, suffer for art). After we found our parking spot, we kids raced out to the playground completely unembarrassed about being in pjs because all the other kids were in their pjs, too: cowboys pajamas, ruffly pink baby doll pajamas, boys wearing their dad's t-shirts that came down to their knees, you saw it all. When the sky started darkening, the commercials would come on, interspersed with an image of a clock showing how much time was left before the show. "Tangy hot pizza!" the announcer would say. "Ice-cold Coca Cola!" It was a bid to get everyone to go to the snack bar, where the food was both terrible and irresistible, and we hardly *ever* got to go so naturally I really wanted to go.

But. There we kids were, running around the playground at breakneck speed, hogging the little platform at the top of the slide, because then you felt like King of the Playground, making the teeter-totter jump, helping push the merry-go-round, difficult to do wearing slippers, and then: MOVIE TIME. We'd race back to the car and settle in, and think, Oh boy we can stay up *really late*, but then we fell asleep pretty quickly.

Cut to the teen years. Many of us got in free by

hiding in someone's trunk. Many of us went on dates to the drive-in and we never saw much of the movie because we were too busy making out. For the boys it was a question of how much they could get. For the girls, it was a question of how far we would let them go. I found it nerve-wracking. There you were in the middle of a great kiss and here would come the wandering hands and your antenna would go up and you would have to make difficult decisions. The boys were in Paradise and the girls were at summit conferences. One night a guy who wanted to go farther than I wanted him to, said, "Come on, I'm going to blow a gasket!" I asked what the heck a gasket was, and that spoiled the mood pretty well.

My tastes leaned toward preppy guys in high school, but the best date I ever had was with this guy I met at Steak and Shake who was practically a gangster. He pulled into the parking lot of the S&S in a chartreuse-colored sports car with BARF written on the side in yellow spray paint. You can see why I was instantly attracted to him. I guess I liked how boldly unconventional he was, driving around in jeans and a t-shirt, his blond hair hanging in his eyes. We had one date, and he took me to the drive-in. I was very disappointed when he came to pick me up because he had greased his hair back and cleaned up and was driving a different car, but never mind, off we went to the drive in and he produced a six-pack of beer which I declined and he did not, and then we made out the whole time and he was and is the best kisser I ever met, ever. I went home with lips swollen to about three times their normal size and I never saw him again.

Sometimes I wonder what was best, going to the drive-in as a kid or as a teenager. I guess I'd have to say as a kid. The pink clouds, the setting sun, the notion that you could be wild on the playground and then run to the safety of a kind of home furnished with an air mattress and a light summer blanket, your parents sitting up in the front and all you could see was the back of their heads but you were pretty sure they were holding hands. It was a summer night, the stars shone above the big movie screen, your parents were awake and you were asleep and you were all together.

ENDLESSLY

Let's see. How to say this. Today I had a doctor's appointment that required one-and-a-half hours of driving. I listened to a lot of disturbing stories on NPR. Then I turned off NPR and listened to a CD of the singer Duffy singing "Endlessly"—endlessly, as it happened—because I kept pushing the button to play it again and again. Then I turned off the radio and listened to the day, to the sound of traffic and birds and various enterprises. I looked at the blue sky and the imaginary animal clouds, the many kinds of people on the sidewalks, different colored boxcars going by on an overpass, the deep yellow of the Shell station sign, birds all lined up on a lamppost.

It came to me like a kind of wide blanket settling that here we all are, all of us, for this brief little window of time. I think God, as you know and understand Her/Him/It, needs to take us all gently by the shoulders and make us look into Her/His/Its eyes so that we can see something we seem to have forgotten a long time ago. I don't think we should wait endlessly to remember something that might make us gasp, weep, and reform.

FABRIC

I was reminded today of a time my friend Marianne and I went to a huge fabric store, a wonderful place, a paradise, that used to be by my house in Natick, Massachusetts. (The Fabric Place, it was called.) We were in there for a looooooooong time, and when we went to the checkout counter we each had so much fabric piled up in our arms we could hardly see over the top of it.

The woman standing behind Marianne said, "Ohhhhhh, what are you *making*?"

Here's what Marianne said: "Nothing."

She was right. We just wanted all that fabric. For some time. In case. Because it was there and it was beautiful.

I believe we went home and let the dog out and then had a martini and looked at the fabric some more.

It's good to have a lot of loves in your life. Friends. Dogs. Martinis. And fabric.

Shelly, this post is for you.

READINGS AND RECIPES

Yesterday, Bill and I traveled treacherous roads (cars slid off the road and accidents everywhere) to get to Champaign, Illinois, where I did a reading from *Make Someone Happy*. Bill drove and I backseat drove. Here's an example of my helpful commentary: "You know, you're supposed to stay a car length behind what's ahead of you for every ten miles you're going!! Did you know that? Huh? One car length, every ten miles! So if you're going forty miles an hour, four car lengths! Right? Huh?" It's a wonder he didn't throw me out of the car.

I figured very few people would come, and I wouldn't have blamed them one bit if they didn't. But!! 80 people were there, and boy, it was another lovely event. The library knocked themselves out with treats, flowers, gift wrap.....Gloria, an earth angel, helped take care of Homer, who was stationed at the back of the room, where he was a good boy. I was given the most beautiful introduction, too. Thank you so much Champaign Public Library!

At Q&A time, I asked for questions, and one of the first was about recipes. In honor of that woman who asked for a recipe, here's my favorite holiday cake.

CRANBERRY UPSIDE DOWN CAKE

12 ounces cranberries, fresh or frozen
1/2 c. dark brown sugar
1/4 c. freshly squeezed orange juice
1 t. finely grated orange zest
3/4 t. cinnamon
2 eggs, at room temp.
1 c. granulated sugar
1 stick (1/2 c.) unsalted butter
1/4 c. sour cream
1 t. vanilla
1/4 t. kosher salt
1 c. flour

1. Stir together cranberries, brown sugar, juice, zest and cinnamon. Set aside.
2. Beat eggs on high speed until pale, about two minutes.
3. Cascade in granulated sugar (this will make you feel like you're the featured guest on the Food Channel) and beat one minute.
4. Switch to medium speed; beat in butter, sour cream, vanilla and salt. Sprinkle in flour. Mix on low, just until combined.
5. Butter lavishly a 9-inch cake pan. Scrape in cranberry mixture. Cover with cake batter. Bake until fruit bubbles at the edges and a toothpick poked in the cake portion comes out clean.
6. Cool on a rack five minutes. Invert a serving platter onto the cake pan. Give the pan a few sharp raps to loosen any sluggish berries. Using oven mitts, lift off pan. Serve warm or at room temp.

Whipped cream is nice with this.

I brought this to Homer's veterinary office the other day. They loved it, and I love them for taking such good care of our boy.

GIFTS AND GRATITUDE

Chocolates and candies, including chocolate covered cherries, and English toffee and giant-sized turtles and pralines from New Orleans. Cookies. Flowers. Many heart-shaped notes with birthday wishes. A book with an angel carved into the pages. A tiny fabric bag with a little dog and cat inside. A mug saying I LOVE BIG MUTTS. A book of the letters of Groucho Marx. Specialty coffees. Handwritten notes from people who have enjoyed my books. And—you'll never have expected this—a dozen eggs!

These are some of the gifts I was given on the *Make Someone Happy* tour, which ended yesterday. I am grateful for every single gift, and I am especially grateful for the kindness of the libraries and the attendees for being so great about letting Homer the dog come, lie on his blanket, and supervise the proceedings. (He got gifts, too, dog cookies and toys!)

Also, I am grateful to people for caring enough about the written word to come to readings—not only mine, but anyone's. I want all the people who listened to me read know how happy it makes me to feel you are *with* me as I do so. When you laugh, I'm thrilled. And when you wipe away tears, I am, too, although in a different way, that has to do with understanding that I'm not alone in the way I feel about things. And I am enormously gratified by the kind things you say to me in the signing line.

I write because I need to. I write to get things from the inside, out. But I publish to try to connect. When I feel I do, well, that's its own distinct pleasure.

On this tour, Bill, Homer and I drove 800 miles to various libraries to meet the warm and really quite wonderful people there. A couple of times, the roads were not so excellent and on one memorable drive through a blizzard where we passed car after car (and one truck) that had slid off the road, I stared out the windshield composing my own obituary: AUTHOR GREASED ON HIGHWAY BEFORE SHE WAS DONE WRITING BOOKS.

Home now, and blessed (truly, blessed) by the fact that soon I'll be going to California to celebrate my friend Phyllis's 70th birthday, then to Boston to enjoy Hanukkah with my daughter and her family, which includes the crown jewels: three grandchildren.

Then home again to settle back into winter and the writing of another novel. I've done a few pages already. The book opens with a woman washing her supper dishes and looking out the window at a night sky full of stars. Writing this, I'm reminded of something Phyllis once said, after I'd received a book for my birthday. She picked it up, turned to the first page, and said, "Hmm. This looks good. They're having pork chops."

WINTER WALK

When I woke up, it was one degree. One. I thought that was sort of cute, like the weather was *try*ing. However, guess how many times I'm going out today?

Still. My maternal grandmother, whose name was Frieda, and who had the prettiest white hair you ever saw (and if you didn't see it, she'd make sure and point it out to you, in a nice, Minnesota-esque way.) Frieda loved the winter. She asked me once if I did too.

"No!" I said. "I hate the cold!"

And she said, "Hmm. I find it refreshing."

If there's one thing a difference of opinion is good for, it's making you consider your possible close mindedness. So today, when it's a *bit* warmer, I'm going to set out the makings for some hot chocolate, including marshmallows, of course (when I make cocoa, it should be called Hot Marshmallow Drink), and then I'm going to bundle up and take Gabby for a walk for at *least* fifteen minutes.

There is something about extremes. There is something about adversity. Also, when I think about it, there really is something refreshing about winter, the air seems purer, the sky cleaner, and you make those little clouds with every exhalation. (I remember being a kid and loving when it was cold enough so I could pretend I was smoking.)

Also, nature is its usual giving self in winter just as it is in every other season: the squirrels gather beneath the bird feeder like a group of friends out for breakfast at George's diner, the structure of trees is revealed in all its elemental glory, snowflakes of frost are in the corners of windows. You get out there and it's so cold you think you'll die, but then it becomes, if not comfortable, at least bearable. And you feel like you've conquered a little something when you burst back into your house. You may not be an arctic explorer, but by God, you've earned your cocoa.

I put off the walk alluded to in the previous post, put it off and put it off. And then I got busted: someone asked if I'd taken it yet. I will, I said. And then I *had* to. But then Bill came home with the groceries I'd asked him to get for the Spicy Chicken Sausage and Fennel and Roasted Red Pepper Soup I'm making (Oprah's recipe in Costco magazine), and I said, "Should I go for a walk? Or will I die out there?"

"You'll die out there," he said, and went down to the basement "for just a minute," which means he was fast forwarding the hockey game and would be out of commission for one hundred years.

I put the chopped tomato and fennel and olive oil mixture in the oven for roasting and then I asked Gabby if she wanted to go for a walk. Make a face like someone was asking you if you wanted to instantly lose 15 pounds and/or have a million dollars. That's the face Gabby showed me. So I put on my Uggs and two scarves and my warmest coat and out we went. It was cold, but there was no wind. Dusk was thinking about descending and the clouds were pink and that reminded me of a story I've told many times, but maybe you haven't heard it. A little girl was out at the end a long walk she'd taken with her family. Her father said, "Want me to carry you home?" The girl said, "No, thanks. Every time I see pink clouds, I don't feel tired."

Smoke was coming out of some chimneys like a picture postcard or a Hallmark movie. There were many Christmas trees at the curb, all undressed now and slated for the pyre, but many of them—in fact, really *all* of them—were still in good shape. *That* reminded me of the time I was nine, and my best friend Carol Cornish and I built a teepee out of Christmas trees. It was a very fine dwelling until it collapsed which it did right around the same time it was being built.

Kudos to the Uggs people: barefoot in my boots, my feet did not get cold. But to the makers of my gloves: Uh, may I see you in the kitchen? Privately?

TWEETING

I was once at a meeting with publishing people. This was quite a while ago. Years ago. They said,

"Do you tweet?"

I said, "Um....You mean, like, talk to people? Like birds talk to each other?"

They explained what a Twitter account was, and suggested I get one.

"Sure, sure," I said. But I never did get one.

This morning I looked at some tweets and the level of disrespect and verbal violence was appalling. I felt like I was walking along the sidewalk and the sidewalk opened up and I fell into hell.

Therefore I have decided not to get a Twitter account but rather share with you an "argument" Bill and I had yesterday about whether Fritzi, our parakeet, should "watch" red carpet fashion with me or hockey with Bill.

"He doesn't like hockey," I said, and Bill said, "He loves hockey!"

"Nuh uh," I said. "He likes fashion."

Bill said, "Listen to his tweets and you'll get his real opinion."

MOUSE PARTY

This post was going to be about old boyfriends. But. Bigger news.

I found mouse poop by my trash can beneath my kitchen sink. I cleaned it up and left a note telling the mice they were evicted. In a nice way.

This did not work.

Next, I got a cheap humane trap and set out a feast inside it. Feast meaning peanut butter. The peanut butter disappeared, the mice did not. The mice sent out an Evite to all their friends, telling them to come to a peanut butter party and the friends happily accepted.

"This is it," Bill said. "We're going to have to kill them."

"Really?" I asked.

Bill assumed the clenched jaw look of a determined John Wayne. I said nothing, but my heart was breaking a little bit. The mice's little round ears. That they were made and appeared on the earth only to have their necks snapped in a trap. Or to have their leg caught in one, and *then* what? They're looking up at you in pain and you say, "Hold on, buddy, I'm going to help you out by killing you *another* way. This will be better! You'll see!"

So we go to the hardware store and Bill gets the old-fashioned traps and we wait in line and just when we reach the cashier, I say, "But....can't we just *try* another humane one?"

Bill, a softie himself, sighs and goes and gets one of those deluxe metal mouse hotels. And we put some more peanut butter in. And the next day, voila. A house mouse party; a whole bunch of them are trapped in there.

"How many?" I ask, and Bill says, "You can look in," and he himself looks in the little window and starts counting them by using his pointer finger like little kids do.

"Where should we let them go?" I ask and I'm afraid I'm a little more excited than the situation warrants. I feel like the dogs when they hear the words "car ride." I feel like when I'm in the depths of a terrible depression and I go and buy a lipstick and chat up the drug store cashier and the depression goes away, just like that.

My vote is to take the mice for a car ride and let them go in the woods. Bill draws himself up to say, "They'll die out there!"

I'm not so sure, I think they'd survive out there, but we compromise by Bill taking them to a big field so they can be field mice. And I feel so much better. When Bill comes back, I say, "Were they happy? Did they all get out their cell phones to call and let their relatives know they're okay?" Bill just smiled and put more peanut butter in the party room.

My guess is that the mice got out their cell phones all right, in order to text my address to all their friends so they know where to come tonight. I suppose I'd better go to the party store and get some tiny little balloons and streamers. Maybe I can get a mouse DJ on short notice.

Before Bill took the mice to let them go, he said, "Want to get a big aquarium and keep them?" I hesitated only the littlest second before I said no.

I think I need to tell you that I *will* kill a centipede. It's their fault for having too many legs. But I'm working on my compassion, I'm always working on my compassion, so who knows, I may have to create dance classes for them: tap-tap-tap-tap-tap dancing.

[Thanks for all your help with my mouse problem. Bill calls the humane trap "reform school."]

LETTER FROM A CENTIPEDE

To: The Pompous and Ignorant Elizabeth Berg

From: The Department of Public Relations for
        Centipedes (DPRC)

Dear Ms. Berg,

Well, well, well. Aren't we quick to disparage things we obviously know very little about? If you can spare the time, permit me to enlighten you about a few things.

You say centipedes have too many legs. As you might know, the term "centipede" implies a hundred legs and many benighted people such as yourself think that we have that many legs. We have a lot, it's true, and that is why we are the world's fastest arthropod. Indeed, scientists complain that we're hard to collect and research because we run so fast our legs fall off. But then we regrow them. Can you do that?

But the average house centipede has only thirty legs. Hardly one hundred, I think you'd agree. Or one thousand, as some really nutso members of your species have attested.

I will agree that you have reason to fear us, but not because we are ugly. Ugly is in the eyes of the beholder. I'm thinking of a certain creature, species homo, variety sapiens, that has nose hairs and has to clip its toenails, okay? I'm thinking of things like warts and cellulite and pimples. I mean, stop me now.

You should fear us not because of how we look or move but because we can be fierce. Let me describe for you the way we eat our victims:

we pounce on them and ensnare them with our back legs, envenom them, and then hold them with our front legs to eat them. We can hold four victims or more at time, so we can eat one victim now and save the rest for later, is that not smart? And we share! When we eat spiders, we eschew their feet, and leave them for you. Also, you know how you guys make happy movements when you eat? We do that too: while eating, we flutter our legs. Really, all centipedes should audition for the Joffrey ballet.

Your William S. Burroughs said that any person who might consider petting a centipede is a traitor to the human race. But we help with decomposition when we eat dead plant matter. And some of us can glow in the dark—can you? We're clean; we always groom ourselves after we eat—do you? Finally, we don't say EWWWWWW when we see you, we don't gossip, and we don't run for political office. I'd say that's enough to raise us in your estimation, wouldn't you?

I thought so.

Sincerely yours,

Hairy Slitherby

Hairy Slitherby

GABBY

Gabby: Um, it is precisely 25 minutes after the time to feed the dogs.

Me: When did you learn to tell time?

Gabby: ....I didn't. Homer told me.

Me: Well, I'm coming.

Gabby: No, you're not. You're typing! That's all you do! You are not a full person! You are wiggling fingers, and that's ALL.

Me: Hmmm. Sounds like someone's hungry.

Gabby: You THINK? And by the way, I think I know what you're going to write about and I am INNOCENT.

Me: ....

Gabby: I AM!!!!!!!!!!!

Me: OKAY! Do you want roast beef or cheese?

Gabby: Both, both and both.

CARDINAL STORY

I looked out into the back yard this morning and saw Gabby with something red. I thought, oh my god, she got a bird! And I yelled GABBY! She came toward me and then I saw that it was a toy. Or I should say I thought it was a toy. But it was, in fact, a cardinal. Immobile.

I was devastated. Gabby has never gone after birds. Had this bird gotten injured another way and then Gabby found it? No way to know. But I told Bill that a bad thing had happened, and there was a dead cardinal in the yard, could he dispose of it? I didn't want to do it.

When Bill went out to do the sorrowful deed, he found that the bird was still alive, and he called to me to tell me so.

"What should we do?" I asked.

Bill didn't know.

"Bring him in, and I'll call someone," I said.

I put a towel in a little box and brought the bird into my office and put him in a corner where he could hide from me or see me, whichever he preferred. I did a quick inspection: no obvious puncture wounds, no bleeding, but the bird was immobile. I called my vet, then an exotic animals vet, who told me to keep the bird warm and quiet, he was probably in shock, and then if he roused, put him out again.

I turned on my space heater to make it warm and cozy and went to work. After about an hour, I walked over to the box and the bird took a few steps. I found some cardinal calls on the computer which I played for him and he seemed to like that.

After another hour, he hopped out of the box. I thought, Great! I let him roam around for a while—he liked settling into the warm and fuzzy dog bed—and then I put him in the box to take him outside. He was pretty peppy by then. But when I put him out, he stayed perfectly still again. He looked up at me. I said to myself, don't you dare anthropomorphize. This is not a Disney movie. He is not thinking of you as his new mom. I had put his box down in order for him to hop out it, and you know what happened? After he walked around a little bit outside, he hopped back *in* the box!

I thought okaaaaay, and I brought him in for a while longer, gave him seed and a little dish of water. Then, after he was walking around again, I put him outside.

I watched from the window as he ate a bit from what had fallen from the bird feeder. Then he moved to the fence, then under it to the neighbor's yard. Then: nothing.

Another cardinal flew down, as if to check on him. Nothing.

After a while, I went back out and the bird was huddled close to the ground, immobile, puffed out and miserable looking. So I brought him back in.

I think he just might need a little more time, and then in the morning I can see about letting him go. But I'm worried he can't fly, that something must have happened to a wing, or both of them. So I'll call a nature center and see what they advise.

Meanwhile, he has been a great roommate: quiet, cooperative, and very beautiful. And utterly appreciative of bird song.

Gabby: I did NOT hurt that bird. It was hurt when I found it. And I thought it was a toy. Who wouldn't think it was a toy? And now I have been kept out of Elizabeth's study ALL DAY. You think life is easy around here? No, it's not.

I left a nightlight on in my office, and in the night got up to check on the bird. He was so quiet. He'd moved into the corner of the laundry basket I had put him in for the sake of the higher walls. He had been very still since I brought him in that last time, and it made me wonder if he had hurt himself more when he'd been out that time, or even if the other cardinal that I thought was trying to help him, hurt him. But he was still breathing.

This morning, I took my time going downstairs, because I feared he had died. And I was thinking that I would spend a little time with him if he had, thanking him silently for his place in the world, for the gift of beauty he brought to anyone who chanced to see him. I wanted to think about how he seemed to want to come back inside with me, that he recognized that I was trying to help him. And I wanted to remember that he lifted his head to hear the sound of his own species, feeling not so alone.

He is alive. But again, very still. He has moved from the corner of the basket to the center. He has eaten a bit. I spoke to him. I put the cardinal sounds back on. Very, very still. I reached down to try to very gently stroke the top of his head, and he said, "HEY! Don't touch me!" so I didn't try that any more.

Right now, he is more awake, listening to the birds, and I am going to call Trailside Nature Center to see if they'll take him. If he can live there, I will visit him as often as I can. If they say he must be euthanized, I will nod, and go home, and—only an animal lover will understand this—I will miss him so much.

This morning, I took the beautiful cardinal—who has become quite energetic!—to The Willowbrook Wildlife Center. I think his right wing is injured, it's hanging lower than the left. I hope they can help him. Gulp.

First, I warmed up the car, including the car seat. Then I told him what was up, he who was moving around really well in his laundry basket. I put a towel over the top of the basket and brought him out to the car and put in the CD I'd brought. We were hitting the road, just like in Easy Rider, except we were in a pretty sedate SUV and our music was not Steppenwolf's "Born to be Wild," but rather "Bird Calls from the Northeast," or something like that. It was a lovely CD, bird calls and other sounds too: rain, crickets, what sounded like a brook running. I was feeling very anxious and so I did what I do when I'm anxious, which is eat. I pulled into a McDonald's drive thru for a breakfast sandwich and coffee and orange juice and the smell of the coffee was comforting and the sandwich was nice and salty.

The bird, who has higher standards and healthier eating habits than mine, took a pass.

When we got to the center, the woman behind the desk took him right in. I teared up a little and asked my birder friend Diann, who had met me there, "Am I not going to see him again?" and she said, "I'm afraid not."

Well.

Over my dead body, thought I.

I peeked through the door and saw pieces of the woman tending to "my" bird. When she came out, Diann spoke up for me.

"She would like to say goodbye to the bird," she said, about me. The woman was very nice, but said no, explaining that the cardinal was now in a quiet zone to reduce stress. He would be kept in dim light, with a heating pad that he could be on or off, his choice. He would be examined soon.

"If you can't help him, can I have him back?" I asked. The woman very kindly told me no. Apparently it's against the law to have a wild bird in captivity in your house.

There was a squirrel in line ahead of Mr. Cardinal: they thought he'd gotten into rat poison. They were going to look at him first. Then they'd let me know about the bird.

So Diann and I had a good look at all the rescued animals housed there, beautiful birds who for one reason or another can't survive in the wild—turtles, some fish, a snake or two, and bobcat who can do tricks, which he loves to do. We had just finished up when the woman who had admitted the cardinal came out to tell me that his wing was not broken, but he did seem to have some neurological damage. When they tried to "perch" him, he listed to the side. Also, there was some swelling near his wing. So they gave him some pain medicine and they'll let him rest a couple of days and see where they are.

"Did the person who took care of him notice how much prettier he is than any other cardinal?" I asked.

She smiled, which I assume meant "He/She sure did!"

So I left him there. His number is 31. I guess that's kind of his name. I'm going to call and see how old 31 is doing tomorrow. They said to wait a couple of days, but I can't.

After I left, I felt terrible. So I went and bought a new car. A 2016 VW Beetle. It was on sale at a big discount. I needed to get rid of my old car (too old and starting to fail) and I thought, what the heck. I'll buy a car. It's better than eating all day. It TOOK ALL DAY to buy the car. And that is why it took me so long to tell you about Mr. Cardinal, who I hope is warm and as comfortable as possible and on the mend. I've thought about him ten thousand times today and as I was washing some dishes after I came home, I wondered if he thought about me. Probably not. But maybe he did. Maybe he thought, that was a fun road trip. We'll have to do it again. She can drive, and I'll fly high above her, but I'll keep her always in my sight.

This morning, Bill and I went to the Church of Beethoven, and listened to a tenor sing Norwegian and Swedish and French opera. This was followed by the reading of two poems, lovely ones. And that was followed by two minutes of silence: the lights dimmed, all sat still and held a deep silence that was shared and yet uniquely individual. And THAT was followed by more singing.

Next we went for lunch for the most fabulous tacos in the world (La Parrillita, on North and Harlem, Oak Park). We made plans to see a movie this evening in one of those lounge-chair theaters that I love so much. We bought new dog dishes and some dog toys and a new orthopedic bed for Homer, and some light bulbs that required going to the hardware store, and if there's one thing I like to do it's go to the hardware store—the guys who work there know everything.

When we got home, I was just about to give the dogs their new toys when I thought, I'm calling about the cardinal.

Okay.

Let me say, first, how much I have loved all your messages about this bird, this little journey we all had with him. I read your comments early in the morning and late at night and I was grateful for every one of them. To you who have been with me in all this, I am sorry as I can be to tell you that the bird died last night.

I wept, of course. I wept and I told Bill, I should have kept him. I shouldn't have put him through the trauma of going somewhere else. He was walking around! He was getting better!

But....you know. The bird died.

And so now I am stopping crying and remembering that this morning I heard beautiful music and poetry. That I will go the picture show later. That these ups and downs, this is life.

Mostly, though, I am thanking that little red bird for all the joy and tender feelings he evoked in so many, and I am looking forward to spring, when baby cardinals will be born again.

NO POTATOES

Home from beautiful Mill Valley, California. On the plane on the way home, I sat next to a very elegant Japanese man. Very nicely dressed, very quiet, sat with wonderful posture the whole time. We did not speak except for the time I got up and said, "Excuse me, please," and he stood to let me pass. I could see him eating out of the corner of my eye and his manners were exquisite. He crossed his silverwear in the manner of Europeans when he had finished, then refolded his napkin. He was watching a movie on his little airplane screen, I was reading a book (Lydia Peelle's exquisite short story collection, *Reasons for and Advantages of Breathing*), and looking up occasionally to see what was happening on my little screen where first C-Span and then HG TV played, soundlessly. I don't have ear buds or earphones or whatever you need to listen and— get this—*I was too shy to ask the flight attendant for them.* Good Lord, I've made no progress at all from the time when I was a little girl at my Aunt Lala's table and she asked if I'd like more of her always divine mashed potatoes. Of course, I wanted more mashed potatoes, I always want more mashed potatoes, but I couldn't say that, I just couldn't say yes, please, because I thought it might be greedy/rude. So I would say, very softly, "I don't care," and she would be properly befuddled and most times I got the potatoes anyway.

But.

At the end of the flight, as we stood to deplane, the Japanese man said, "I like your red glasses."

"Oh!" I said. "Thank you! They're just readers I got from the drugstore."

"Very cute," he said, and then we just beamed at each other. And I thought, Jeez. We should have had a conversation during that long flight. But he was too shy and I was too shy and so neither of us got any potatoes.

IT CAN'T BE *THAT* GOOD

Not long ago, my daughter Jenny sent me a recipe for a soup that she said she and her husband both loved. I filed it away to try. Then my other daughter Julie tried it, and was *raving* about it. So the other night, I tried it, and now I'm going to rave about it too.

It will look simple to you, and it is simple to prepare. It will seem like such common ingredients, and the ingredients are indeed common. (You can substitute ground turkey or TVP for the ground beef, although I used ground beef this first time). You will think, hmmm. It can't be *that* good. But it is! And it's low-cal! And filling! And great for winter, especially when you serve it with great crunchy rolls, all heated up and buttered.

Oh jeez, now I might have to make it again tonight.

BEEF, CABBAGE AND TOMATO SOUP

1 pound lean ground beef (or ground turkey or TVP)
1 1/2 t. Kosher salt
1/2 c. diced onion
1/2 c. diced celery
1/2 c. diced carrot
1 28-oz. can crushed tomatoes
5 c. chopped green cabbage (many supermarkets sell this already chopped, a great convenience)
4 c. beef stock, canned or homemade (can use vegetable broth)
2 bay leaves

1. Heat Dutch oven and then grease with oil.

2. Add ground beef and salt and cook until browned, about 3-4 minutes.

3. Add onion, celery and carrots and sauté 4-5 minutes.

4. Add tomatoes, cabbage, stock and bay leaves, and cook covered on low to medium heat for 40 minutes.

Great for lunch the next day!

Thank you Jenny and Julie!

THE MOTH

Running around town doing errands, and The Moth comes on the radio. I hear such interesting stories, all of them really quite wonderful. One is about the woman who became hairdresser to David Bowie. One is about a guy whose girlfriend breaks up with him, he takes a job walking dogs in a shelter, and comes to meet Lake, a dog who has been there for two years....The last one I heard was from a refugee from Africa named Abeny Kucha. It made me feel like bawling and cheering simultaneously.

Ellen Gilchrist said, "Compassion and wisdom are already with us. But we have to spread the word of good things."

So I am doing that by telling you about these stories. Please find some time, get some tea, some cocoa, a glass of wine, a martini, milk and cookies or whatever you want. Sit down, Google the stories, close your eyes and listen—at least to Abeny's story. You will not be disappointed. You will be reminded of the value of storytelling. And of heart. And compassion. And sharing. Of being human. Of the deep meaning of home.

STAMPS

My father had a hobby that embarrassed me to no end when I was a teenager. (Of course, when I was a teenager everything embarrassed me. Someone shaking catsup from a bottle, for example.) Anyway, he collected stamps. Or, as I thought of it then, he collected *stamps*!!!!!!!!! He sent off for a lot of mint stamps, and he also used to soak ones he didn't have and found interesting or beautiful off corners of envelopes in a little bowl of water. Then he would use flat-ended tweezers to lift them off and let them dry before mounting them. One of my memories of living at home was seeing that bowl of water on the kitchen counter, a stamp being gradually loosened so that it could be adopted by a man who appreciated it.

Cut to many years later. Many. I am standing in line at the post office and craning my neck around the person ahead of me to see if I can tell what stamps are available today. Recently, I bought a sheet of birds, and one of pets. I bought one of trucks that I like so much I can hardly stand to use the stamps. On this day, I see that I can buy Chinese New Year stamps featuring (oh, be still my chicken-loving heart) a rooster! So I mail my package and I buy some beautiful red and gold and chickeny stamps and I can hardly wait to affix them to envelopes so that I can look at them again.

Here is the way I pay bills: I put on some wonderful music, jazz or classical or sometimes 40s big band. I get out my favorite fountain pen and if possible use turquoise ink. I use a completely different penmanship than I usually do, just for fun. And then, the big moment: I put a stamp on the bill.

This late in life, I, too, have come to love stamps. I don't collect them, but I appreciate that they are little tiny works of art that serve a practical purpose. And these days, whenever I think of that little bowl of water, with stamps coming loose, I feel a great tenderness.

Would that I had felt that way, then. And said so.

Ah well. Lessons for the living: the show always ends sooner than you think it will, for you and for others. But love finds lots of ways to express itself, and it is our great fortune that we have an opportunity every day to pull ours out like magicians' scarves.

READING THE NEWSPAPER

Teresa Crawford captures the moment.

VALENTINE'S DAY

When I was a kid, we decorated shoe boxes to hold our valentines. Kleenex carnations, lots of pink and red crepe and construction paper, pipe cleaner sculptures.... Then we lined the boxes up on the windowsill of the classroom to await delivery. When it was time for our Valentine's Day party, we sat at our desks and ate cupcakes and cookies and drank punch and opened our cards. Two things:

1. I believed every valentine. I believed each one was personally selected for me. Oh, Tommy has a crush on me! Doug, too! Oh, look, Cindy has a crush on me, too!

   That was in my private, hopeful glitter heart. In my real heart, I feared no one would like me ever until the end of time. I feared this until I was about 40.

2. I wonder if the teachers liked all the parties we used to have. Or if they just liked nap time best.

HAPPY VALENTINE'S DAY!

May you receive lots of Valentines. And just remember, a dog walking by with his tail wagging is a valentine.

GOOD SOUP

I'm going to paste this recipe here because it's so easy and so *good*. I used Trader Joe's spicy chicken sausages and just sliced them up. Also added a few onions I had oven roasted until they were really crisp. Use all the garlic; it's not overpowering at all. Loved the Parmesan in here. We gobbled this up. It's from *Taste of Home*. Oh jeez, now I want to make it *again*.

RUSTIC ITALIAN TORTELLINI SOUP

Makes 6 servings

3/4 pound Italian turkey sausage links, casings removed
1 medium onion, chopped
6 garlic cloves, minced
2 cans (14-1/2 oz. each) reduced-sodium chicken broth
1-3/4 c. water
1 can (14-1/2 oz.) diced tomatoes, undrained
1 package (9 oz.) refrigerated cheese tortellini
1 package (6 oz.) fresh baby spinach, coarsely chopped
2-1/4 t. minced fresh basil or 3/4 t. dried basil
1/4 t. pepper
Dash crushed red pepper flakes
Shredded Parmesan cheese, optional

Crumble sausage into a Dutch oven; add onion. Cook and stir over medium heat until meat is no longer pink. Add garlic; cook one minute longer. Stir in the broth, water and tomatoes. Bring to a boil.

Add tortellini; return to a boil. Cook for 5-8 minutes or until almost tender, stirring occasionally.

Reduce heat; add the spinach, basil, pepper and pepper flakes. Cook 2-3 minutes longer or until spinach is wilted and tortellini are tender.

Serve with cheese if desired.

Freeze option: Place individual portions of cooled soup in freezer containers and freeze. To use, partially thaw in refrigerator overnight. Heat through in a saucepan, stirring occasionally and adding a little broth if necessary.

Originally published as Rustic Italian Tortellini Soup in *Healthy Cooking*, October/November 2008, p33.

NAPPING

I was maybe four or five. I'm not sure where I was living, because we moved around so much, but I know I was in a kitchen, near a table. The grown-ups were talking about why I was protesting taking a nap. I had to think about this for a minute. And then I realized that I hated taking a nap because: 1) I wasn't sleepy, and 2) If I went up to take a nap, I might miss something.

Well, don't the years change things, though. I love naps now. I have a little nap ritual, which is that I bring a glass of cold water to the bedside, I close the shutters in my bedroom, I fluff up the pillows and read for a while, and then I lie under either a quilt that someone made me, or a blanket that someone gave me, and I drift off. It is like drifting, too. It's like being dandelion fluff riding the wind. And it turns out that it's nice to miss a few things, to shift into neutral and fall back into a benign state of nothingness to let the world go on without you. And then come back into the world in the way that waking up from a nap has you do. It's like the opposite of goodnight moon: hello, window. Hello, light in the late afternoon sky. Hello dresser holding photos of animals and people I love. Hello, dog at the bedside, hello kitchen where I go downstairs to put on a CD and start dinner, full of goodwill toward just about everything, because of a nap. I have a good idea. Let's all of us oldsters have little kids tuck us in, and let them stay up and keep an eye on things. More and more, I feel that young children, full of optimism and trust and energy and willingness, are better able to be trusted than anyone.

PUPPIES AND OTHER THINGS

This is a big apology to the people who have taken time to send me a note or a letter in care of my publisher. Publishers are notoriously late in sending along author mail. Yesterday, I got a big pack of letters, all of which were old, some nearly a *year* old. So I'm very sorry for those of you who wanted or needed attention earlier. Out of my control, unfortunately.

I also received an unsolicited manuscript, which I am unable to read or even look at, for legal reasons. Please be reminded that I cannot look at *any* unsolicited manuscripts.

Otherwise, the day is going swimmingly. I have the ingredients to make date bars, which I have been craving. (I always feel I should be wearing a '40's suit complete with hat and gloves and nylon stockings with seams when I eat them, so old fashioned are they.) Also, Homer, my nearly 14-year-old Golden, apparently believes that he is young again. He trotted beside me this morning like he was in the ring at Westminster, his scraggly old tail high and wagging. (I do brush him, but that tail is beyond hope) May I have one billionth of his heart and spirit and willingness and tendency toward joy if I reach MY nineties.

Whenever spring comes, I want a puppy. I hope I have the strength to keep off puppy websites today.

And now, if you'll excuse me, I'm going to go and look at puppy websites.

LITTLE EMERGENCIES

I think the best writing comes from that sense of emergency, that feeling that what you are trying to say is larger than anything you or anyone else might say about it. This emergency/feeling is not in need of anyone else's opinion, including your own; and it does not accommodate or react to emotions like fear or desire, it is independent of all that. And it is unstoppable, it must be born, you cannot rest until you get out what is suddenly ready to boil over. Interestingly, I think things can percolate inside of us unconsciously, and it's only when they reach the boil-over state—the emergency state—that we can get out of our own way and let what needs to happen, happen in the most authentic way possible.

As for now, it is a cloudy Sunday; in mid-afternoon, the house lights need to be on. And I am going to sit under lamplight and read. And then I am going to sit in the quiet and think about what I've just read. It seems like so long since I've done that. That's because it's been so long since I've done it.

I believe there are times in our lives that are little emergencies, when we see that the balance has shifted too far in one direction or the other, and parts of ourselves need more care and feeding than we've been willing to give. I need to spend less time on the computer and more time under the lamplight, so that I can learn better how to see.

SEEING THE LIGHT

I took Gabby for a long walk. In a park, I saw a man, maybe 70, with what I assume was his granddaughter, maybe four. The man was singing to beat the band. The granddaughter was standing before him, leaning against his knees, and she couldn't stop smiling. I started smiling, too, and for all I know Gabby, too, was trotting along with a grin on her face.

I like to hear people talk about random memories in a stream-of-consciousness kind of way. It hardly every happens, but when it does, it's magical to me: it's as though the essence of someone is coming out of them like ticker tape. I'll bet when that little girl grows up, if she's asked to share random memories, she'll put that into the mix:

"And I remember one day when my Grandpa took me to the park and we were watching all the people and Grandpa was singing loud, and everybody who went by, smiled." I can imagine her adding, "And I thought that was how the world *was*, can you imagine?"

Well, the world may not be like that, but here's what I think: turn people often enough toward the light and they begin to see light. See it, trust in it, and reflect it back.

A SMARTER KIND OF LOVE

When I was about twelve, I started using nature as an antidote to all kinds of things. I would go out for a walk in the fields near the Army base in Germany where we were living and return calmer, more grateful, more optimistic, and informed by things all around me: mighty trees, rich black earth, wildflowers, butterflies, clouds. There was a grounding quality to being outside like that. I feel in nature a kind of benign indifference that feels like a smarter kind of love, if you know what I mean.

Today, I read the paper because I feel I must. The usual reaction occurred: anxiety. Despair. Oh, and a kind of wonderment about a recipe for lasagna that was waaaaaaay too complicated. But the lasagna recipe did little to help the sadness. And so I watched the nature video I get as an email every day. It showed a forest, tall pine trees standing still and stately in a snowstorm, and all was quiet, and the quiet was a balm.

I hate the cold, but I loved watching this. Sometimes the greatest eloquence is in silence.

OBITS

"Well! I wasn't expecting *this*," I told Bill, after bursting into tears at the breakfast table.

Let me back up just a bit.

It is my habit to read the obits every now and then. I see them as consolidated and illuminating life stories that do a lot for letting me know someone I never knew. I think it's important for us to know each other generally, and obits provide a daily window into our species.

But the other day, the obit was for a very young man, around 18 years old. I contemplated cutting and pasting the obit, but it seemed that would be overstepping some boundary that I want to honor. So let me just say that this young man was born with disabilities that meant he could never eat apart from being tube fed, but that his favorite job in his school was helping with food prep for others. The obit said right at the start that this notice was meant to celebrate a life that, though short, was well-lived, and to celebrate as well a beautiful death: a person in a room with a glorious view, under a blanket that had sentimental meaning, held by the people who loved him most and who sent him off to that unknown shore with some measure of regret, but mostly with love and everlasting gratitude.

It was so honest, so deeply felt, so brave, in many ways. I would have been moved by that alone. But the biggest thing that got to me, I think, was that in the face of considerable adversity, someone consciously chose the path of love and light seemingly every day of his life.

I feel that we are living in times that assault us every day. I feel that the national mood is dark and despairing. But I also *still* believe that most people are basically good. We get lost sometimes, we get confused, we get combative, but at heart we are basically good.

In the paper today, I saw a photo of a man in a suit (which is to say not a paramedic but probably a passer-by) delivering CPR to someone in London on the day of that horrific attack, and I thought, Well, there you go. There's a man who was called to service at a time of great urgency and he stepped right up. I guess I believe that more people would, than not. That there are more of us who would extend a hand to someone in need than not. If that makes me naive, may I live forever in the land of Naiveté.

So. In this challenging time, here's my mission. To sit each day in meditation, brief though it is, in order to remind myself of the goodness all around me. And to do my best to *make* for goodness around me. It's not always easy. It's often hard. But it's too important not to try.

P.S. After I burst into tears, I showed the obit to Bill, who read it, and then, in a very quiet voice said, "Well. I'm glad you found that."

OUR FUNNY LIVES

I drove for an hour in the rain to get to the doctor's office, listening to jazz on the radio. A couple of times I thought about why I was going and I got nervous. Then I thought, Well, I'm getting older. This is what happens when you get older, you get stuff that makes you go to the doctor more often than you'd like to, and you go with a certain amount of trepidation.

In the waiting room, I opened my book (Karl Ove Knausgaard's compulsively readable *My Struggle.*) and before I had read two paragraphs I was called in. "Well!" I said. "You guys are right on time today!" This was so that I would get good karma back. Also it was because they were right on time.

I went into the little room and changed into the horrible paper gown that is so stupid-looking you should really just stand there naked, that would look better, regardless of how your body looks. *Any* body is better than those scratchy paper gowns that are not even a fun color or pattern, but a solid white that is whiter than white. I thought I would read some more, but the doctor came in right away. We had a conversation. I showed him some stuff. His diagnosis: Aw, that's *nuth*in'.

My stomach unclenched. I thanked him. I told him his skin looked so nice and asked him what he used on his face. "I don't use anything," he said. "It's just genes," he added modestly. And then, "Not fair, huh?" We shared a little laugh and then I floated out into the waiting room.

I drove home in the rain. I stopped at the grocery store for a rotisserie chicken which I ate for dinner along with sautéed spinach and roasted potatoes I had left over. I shared some with the dogs. Then I fed the parakeet and cleaned up the kitchen and every normal activity seemed gilded to me. And then I thought of that Woody Allen movie where's he's really scared he has a brain tumor and he goes to the doctor and he doesn't have a brain tumor and he is ecstatic until he remembers that something else is going to get him.

What funny lives we live, don't we? We are victims of our own self-awareness. For me, the best thing to do is always keep things small and immediate. Don't project into the future. Be grateful for the things at hand. I'm not always good at remembering to do all that. Today, though, after my doctor's visit, I did the grateful thing really well. Now I'm going to go and do it some more. See you.

POETRY

I'm nine years old and living in Ft. Hood, Texas. I have a card table in my room, and that is where I sit when I labor over and finally complete my very first poem. It's called "Dawn," and it's terrible, even for a kid. Last verse:

> *The elves retired*
> *The people woke*
> *The beauty enchantment*
> *Now was broke.*

Okay?

Nonetheless, I sent it to American Girl Magazine, certain they would publish it.

They did not publish it. They sent me a rejection letter that said, "Ew. We reject this piece of crap always and forever." More or less. And I was so devastated I lay on my bed and wept for what seemed like hours though it probably was more like ten minutes and was no doubt followed by a trip to the kitchen where I made a brown sugar sandwich so as to feel better.

I am now 68. On Wednesday night, I read a poem I wrote in front of a large audience. It was at the Poetry Foundation in Chicago, at an evening celebrating Gwendolyn Brooks. All of us who read (and there were many!) had been asked to fashion a poem inspired by a line in one of Brooks' poems. I am sorry to report that my poem was not a whole lot better than the one I wrote when I was nine.

However.

I got off the stage and sat down, and that nine-year-old who still lives in me felt awfully special. It was all I could do to not laugh out loud.

EASTER MEMORY

I'm not sure why some memories stick in our brains, but here is an Easter memory that sticks in mine.

I was eight, living in Minnesota while my Dad was serving in Korea. On Easter morning, I crept downstairs and found my basket hidden on the bookshelf. I brought it upstairs to my bedroom and sat on the floor to inspect the contents. No black jelly beans, that was excellent (although now I love them). Lots of marshmallow eggs, excellent. Peeps, which I was not crazy about, but ate anyway because it was so satisfying to bite their heads off. My favorite thing, though, were the dyed hard-boiled eggs. I cracked them open on my head and then lay on my back to eat them. I have no idea why I did that, and cannot recommend eating this way, as choking is always a possibility.

After I ate most of the things in my basket, I went to look out my bedroom window. My microscope was on the ledge, so that I could catch the sun in the little mirror that provided light to the slides I loved to look at—salt crystals, sugar crystals, a hair off my head that, under the microscope, looked like a log. In those days, I was literally a card-carrying member of the Junior Scientists of America club.

There wasn't much activity outside yet, it was still early, but the light was lovely and I knew that soon people would emerge from their houses wearing their Easter outfits, pastel, scratchy things, beribboned things. Some people even got new shoes and a new purse. I felt sorry for the boys, who only got to wear their dumb suits and ties.

I was raised Catholic, and don't even get me started on the mystery of a mother seeing her son crucified and then being told he had risen from the dead. I spent a lot of time sitting in churches with my eyes wide open, wondering.

I am no longer a scientist in any sense; the field proved too academically challenging for me. But I still spend time with my eyes wide open, wondering. And I still like to bite the heads off of peeps.

Today's menu is carrot ginger soup, ham, Easter potatoes, oven roasted asparagus with garlic and Parmesan, a carrot salad I found in the New York Times that uses roasted carrots, cumin, pomegranate molasses and arugula. I don't know what all else but it sounded too intriguing not to make. I made lemon/lavender butter to put on the rolls.

My mom always used to send me the menu for what she was making for holiday meals. I always loved that. I ate with my eyes. If you read this, may you eat with yours. And may you have a happy Sunday, full of wonder.

LETTERS

I was reading a book recently wherein there was a description of a guy getting ready to read a letter. A real, handwritten letter that came for him in the mail. Remember those?

He had to get ready before he opened the envelope. He had to prepare a cup of tea. He had to light a cigarette. He had to sit himself comfortably at the kitchen table. Only then was he ready to read the letter. I imagined what happened next: He slit the envelope open. Slid out the letter. Unfolded the pages. Noted the ink (or pencil) color, the style of penmanship. Began reading, and was in the presence of another, even though he was sitting there alone.

Boy. I remember how wonderful it used to feel when I got handwritten letters. Maybe they were from my mom, and she would talk about how she didn't have the energy she used to, though it must be said until practically her dying day, she had far more energy than I. Maybe it was from one of my friends. Oh, I got great letters from friends. When I was in college, I corresponded with a priest who took all my philosophical musings and questions seriously, and responded in kind; and I corresponded with a young man who was deeply intelligent and poetic, and had no problem writing me letters that could easily reach eight or nine pages—both sides of the paper covered in his tiny black script.

The letters I got most excited about in college were from my boyfriend, who lived far away; I thought I'd pass out before I got up to my dorm room to lie down and read them. And then read them again. And then read them again.

By the time I was in my mid-twenties and living alone in an apartment, most of my mail was bills. Even then, back in the early '70s, before email, people weren't writing letters so much anymore. A girlfriend come home with me once to hang out, and I stopped at my little black metal mailbox before we went in, and I must have looked into that mailbox like I was trying to peer down into the depths of the deepest ocean. My disappointment was clear, even without my saying, "Jeez. Nobody writes letters anymore."

Well. That friend, whose nickname was rightly "Wonder," began sending me letters, just so when I looked into the mailbox I'd do a little jump of joy instead of looking like the model for Eyeore.

I saved a lot of letters from a lot of people in a little brown suitcase, and I read them now and again, even though I know how dangerous it is to do so. Nostalgia can embrace you too tightly; you can become disoriented and a bit sad, you can want too much to go back to a past you can never have again, and that perhaps never really was, anyway.

I still send letters every now and then. I'm privileged to have been given the most beautiful greeting cards, some with beautiful photos, some even with little quilts!!!! And I think carefully about who to send those cards to because I want them to be appreciated.

But here's the thing: I don't need to think that carefully, because almost everyone appreciates those cards. I got a dear text from my son-in-law, thanking me for a card I'd attached to a movie I'd given him and my daughter. The photo was of a river, and he said how much he liked long exposures of water, they looked so peaceful.

In this time of such speed, such instant-this and instant-that, I think it's even more wonderful than usual to write and receive letters. And so I hereby proclaim this send-a-letter day. Buy a beautiful card or send a note on a ripped-off piece of paper bag. Tell someone that you're thinking of them by telling them what you're up to. It's easier than you think. Just say where you are, what you see, smell, hear. "I'm out on the front porch and the smell of lilacs is in the air, taking me right back to the time when I had a bottle of Friendship Garden on my dresser. Come to think of it, I don't know if it smelled like lilacs, but it should have." Or "I'm at work, secretly writing to you instead of studying spread sheets." Or "Hey! I saw someone standing outside of Starbucks today that looked a bit like you." Or "Good Lord, how long since we had a great talk? Let's go out and talk." Say anything. "I had a dream last night." "Maybe I should have lived in Texas." Real words on real paper. Send someone a letter today with an envelope and a stamp, and just see if they aren't thrilled. It doesn't have to be long. It doesn't have to brilliant or insightful. It just needs to be you, tapping someone on the shoulder and saying, "Surprise!" If you send someone a letter, they will be surprised. And I'll bet you ten bazillion dollars they'll smile. If they don't, don't try to collect on this bet. I don't have ten bazillion dollars and if I did it would only make me unhappy.

Hey. I guess this is my letter for today to you. Happy spring, happy lilacs, happy memories.

Love, Elizabeth

LITTLE BUDDHA

I've been reading quotes by my seven-year-old grandson, who is a little Buddha. I love this one: "Today might not be the best. But tomorrow might be. You always have a chance."

SUNRISE SUNSET

I'm off today to a wedding in SF. My friend
Marianne's son. Good lord. I remember him as a
newborn. As a little boy being introduced to
sweet/sour candy by yours truly. And now he's
the handsomest, kindest, most optimistic man.
Beautiful couple, such happiness from seeing a
beautiful couple start their lives. Who doesn't love
a wedding? I happen to know, too, that after it's
all over, Marianne and I are going to have yellow
cake and martinis. For dinner. I might have to get
out of my seat on the plane and get out and push
it to make it go faster.

MEATLOAF!

Here's what I'm making for dinner. Maybe you want to make it, too, and we'll all pretend we're sitting at the same table, which I wish we were. We'd need a loooooooong table, but wouldn't we have fun?

MINI TURKEY MEATLOAVES WITH CHILI GARLIC GLAZE

Active Time: 20 minutes. Total Time: 1 hour. Serves: 6

For the glaze:
½ c. rice wine vinegar
6 T. honey
¼ c. soy sauce
3 T. toasted sesame oil
2 T. Asian chili garlic paste, plus more to taste
2 cloves garlic, minced
¼ t. salt

For the meatloaf:
Vegetable oil, for pan
2 lbs. cold ground turkey
2 c. fresh white breadcrumbs
2 eggs, lightly beaten
1 T. peeled and minced fresh ginger
1 T. Asian chili garlic paste
1½ c. roughly chopped cilantro
10 scallions, trimmed and finely chopped
2 T. soy sauce
2 T. toasted sesame oil
2 T. hoisin sauce
4 cloves garlic, crushed
1 t. salt
½ t. freshly ground black pepper

For the garnish:
2 T. black or white sesame seeds, or combination
Chopped cilantro

1. Preheat oven to 400 degrees. Line a baking sheet with parchment paper.
2. Make glaze: Bring vinegar, honey, soy sauce, sesame oil, chili garlic paste, garlic and salt to a boil in a medium saucepan over medium-high heat. Once liquid comes to a boil, decrease heat to low and simmer until mixture thickens enough to coat the back of a spoon, about ten minutes. Remove from heat.
3. Meanwhile, make meatloaf: In a large bowl, combine all ingredients and mix well but lightly, using your hands or a fork.
4. Divide meat mixture into six equal portions and shape each into a small loaf. Place on prepared baking sheet. Use a spoon to make a small indentation in top of each loaf. Spoon a tablespoon of glaze over each loaf. Reserve remaining glaze for later use.
5. Place meatloaves in oven. Bake, using a meat thermometer to monitor temperature, until internal temperature reaches 155-160 degrees, 25-30 minutes. Remove from oven and spread another spoonful of glaze over each loaf. Set aside five minutes, then transfer to a platter. Sprinkle with sesame seeds and herbs. Serve hot, warm or at room temperature.

TRAIN TRAVEL

I have a great love of riding on trains, but an irrational fear of getting on the wrong train. A huge irrational fear. What could happen? one might ask. Worst case, you get off at the next stop, turn around, and go back to Chicago and start again. Worst case, you arrive late. But in my fear, wrong train translates to....Well, picture your version of hell. Someplace very dark and smoky. Also fire-y. And full of horrible screeching noises of metal on metal so that you want to cover your ears like in that Munch painting "The Scream." And dangerous looking steps that lead up to a dark seat that turns out to be the wrong seat, and there I am, my nose pressed up again the window, terrified and unable to get off.

Therefore, on my last train trip from Chicago to Troy, Michigan, I asked very nicely if my partner, Bill, would escort me to the *right* train. He answered very nicely that he could not. Parking, the need to get back to Homer, etc. etc. all legitimate excuses, but this is what I heard: "I do not care about you at all and I never did and I never will."

Thankfully, I also heard, "It's EASY. Go in the door, go down the escalator, go to the Metroliner Lounge. They'll board right out of there."

So okay. I descended the escalator and there were sixty million signs and I just stood paralyzed until I figured out how to get to customer service. There was a formidable, unsmiling woman sitting behind the desk wearing a most fetching shade of lipstick, a kind of beautiful purple. However, I was not there to admire lipstick. I was there to testify. And so I put my purse on the counter, dug out the thing I had printed off the computer for my trip and said, "I don't know what I'm doing."

She snatched the paper from me and said, "First of all, this is not a ticket."

My heart rate accelerated. See? I was thinking? *See?*

And then she said, "Hold on to your purse."

I agreed that I would.

"I *said*, hold onto your *purse*," she said.

"Oh. You mean, now?"

She looked out at me from the slits her eyes had become.

"You in Chicago now," she said.

And so I reached over for my purse and pressed it to my chest like it was my long-awaited newborn.

"So after I get my ticket I just go to the lounge and they board from there, right?" I said.

"*Wrong*," she said. "They ain't done that for a year. I'll tell you what to do when I give you your ticket. Give me your driver's license."

I gave her my driver's license, and her face changed from rock to paper, if you know what I mean. It softened. She smiled. "Oh, I see you're a Sagittarius," she said. "I'm a Sagittarius, too."

"Sagittarians like each other," I said. Hopefully.

"Yes, they do," she said. "And we generally nice, but if you piss us off too much, look out. Look *out*."

She gave me my ticket and said, "Now this is what you to do to get to the train." She told me all the turns, twice. Slowly. Then she said, "You got time to eat, too. You just leave your suitcase right here and I'll watch it for you. The food court is upstairs. I'll tell you how to get there. There's a McDonalds right at the top of the escalator and a Dunkin donuts, too. You got time, baby."

Reader, I followed her directions and I went up and got a Sausage McMuffin with egg and orange juice even though I know it's bad for me. I can't help it, it tastes so good! Then I went to pick up my bag where it had been ferociously watched over by my new best Sagittarius friend and then I sat at Gate C and waited. And started thinking, But what if this *isn't* the right gate C?

And I asked someone, "Are you on the Wolverine?" And then I relaxed because they said yup, and then I started thinking about what swell names trains have like the Wolverine and the Empire Builder and the Sunset Limited and the Southwest Chief and then it was time to board and I got irrationally happy. Which is much better than having irrational fears.

HUMAN NATURE

I want to ask, as I have before: When will it end, the violence, the shootings, what seems to be an ever-escalating loss of basic civility? When I've asked before, people I respect have answered, "Never. Because of human nature."

Is this human nature? A baby being bathed in a kitchen sink, a toddler bending from the waist to inspect a rose, a kindergartener sitting in story circle, is evil there then?

I just got up from watching CNN to take Gabby for a walk. We had a thunderstorm late this afternoon, and rain was still wet upon lawns and caught in the folds of flowers. Water was dripping from the trees and bushes, and there were puddles in the streets reflecting the sky. There was one cloud that held light, a rose gold light, as though it had captured it and now was showing everyone like kids show you fireflies in a jar.

I let Gabby lead the way, just followed her wherever she wanted to go. She made a neat rectangle, up a few blocks, one over, then a right turn to head back toward home. And I confess that I was glad she didn't want a longer walk because I was afraid to be outside. This though the birds sang their night songs and lamps shone a deep yellow inside the houses and there was an abiding sense of peace and safety. But surely there was a sense of safety on that ball field this morning. And at the UPS office in San Francisco before *that* shooting started.

I just wrote a friend saying I felt ashamed of being a human being. But there is still some

stubborn resistance inside me that says, All right.
It happened again. So now we double down on
the right things. Every misdeed, we meet with a
double dose of kindness and care. What is the
alternative? I have to think that somehow there is
a way to overcome this, to work against it.

Each house I passed, I thought, There. Inside
that place. Is there a person in there going quietly
crazy? Is there a killer in the making? Is there
someone who has a total disregard for life, even
his or her own, who will soon commit some
heinous act that proves it?

I don't know. Everything feels so unsure.
Everything feels so sad and discouraging. And
then I thought about everyone in every house
everywhere coming out to stand on their doorstep
however they are: in aprons or pajamas or t-shirts
and jeans or silk dresses or three piece suits, in
slippers or shoes or barefoot, just come out as
you are right now, and in so doing, be saying, All
right. Enough. I'm here. Let's begin.

I had to think that before coming into my
own house and closing the door against another
day full of the kind of horror we must never get
used to. I have to hope that the biggest part of
human nature is ever on the side of life and love,
and that any day now, we will see the evidence of
that. It will never be perfect, I know, but surely
we can do better than this.

OFFERINGS

I have been reading your responses to my latest post, and I am overwhelmed by the generosity of people who help one another, even when their own pain is bigger than that borne by the one they're comforting. And I am reminded that we always need to help one other, because, as the saying goes, life is like licking honey off a thorn. When I was in nursing school, we were taught never to underestimate the pain of the person who had a minor operation just because the person next to him had a major one. They both needed comfort. Widen the lens: we all need comfort, probably all the time.

Whatever our background, whatever our circumstances, what we have to give each other that means—and helps—the most is love. Look how much of that is offered here.

BIRDSONG

When I lived in Boston, there used to be a radio station that played birdsong as the start to an early morning show. It came on at maybe 6am, and it was lovely to wake up to. I'm sorry to say I don't recall any particulars (who did it, what station it was on) but I do know that the first time I heard it, I thought it was a miracle of some sort. It lasted for a long time, too, way past the length of time that such things are usually offered. So often, something lovely is offered in an abbreviated, rushed form, as if people making the offer feel they only have a few seconds to hold onto someone's attention. Given the extreme distractibility you see in people these days, maybe that's true. But I think things like birdsong (and music and art and poetry) work against that kind of chaos. They are like drinks of water for a parched soul. I subscribe to a daily nature video, and what was offered today reminded me of the worth of holding still for a minute, and just listening to a bird. It is my pleasure to share it here with you: http://nature365.tv/july-6-2017/

BEING HERE

Today, before the big rains and thunder and lightning hit, I took Gabby for a walk. I had just come back when the sky darkened to what looked like night, and the rain began to fall—big heavy drops. There is no feeling quite like the cozy/smug one you get when you *just* miss a storm.

While I was out, I saw yellow school buses practicing their runs for the upcoming school year, I suppose. This was kind of irritating, since it came on the heels of my having seen fall clothes in the store windows on Michigan Avenue yesterday. Fall clothes, when the temperature today is going to be 93!! I would think the women mannequins in the store windows might want to be wearing gauzy little dresses, the men linen pants and chic black t-shirts, sunglasses pushed to the top of their heads; and they could be reclining in porch chairs, fake lemonade on a little table nearby, fake fireflies suspended in the air. Some people might still be looking for bathing suits, you know. And they would have to push past big fat coats to the meager offerings shoved off into a dark corner. I ask you, must we always rob the season of its prime?

But. Truth be told, I'm often robbing moments of their prime because I'm too often focused on what comes next. Slowing down and paying attention is so easy to say and is oftentimes so hard to do. (I get this dramatic visual, thinking of paying attention, someone looking into someone else's eyes and saying, "Are you hearing me? Are you here? *Be* here!")

Ah well, we need reminders for the most important things in life, it seems, and so I'll take seeing that school bus as a reminder not to crowd my brain with thoughts of fall but instead relish the fact that we are mid-summer. Super sweet corn is almost ready, there are red cherries in a blue bowl on my kitchen table, the lines at the ice cream stores are long (nothing like an ice cream store to turn adults into kids), people are up to their navels in lake water and standing with their hands on their hips to take in the glorious sights of green trees in the distance and blue water all around and white clouds and yellow sun over-head. Best of all, the cider donuts at our local farmers' market are many weeks away from being gone. (Notice how I avoid talking about the glorious kale and squash and tomatoes and cheese and instead focus on the donuts.)

I'm going to write a couple of final scenes for my next novel, and then I'm going on the porch for lunch and to watch the rain and listen to the thunder boom. Inside, Gabby will be fretting, almost knocking on the window to say, "What are you *doing?* Get *in* here!" I will only come in if the thunder booms so hard I feel it in my chest. Then I'll cower with Gabby.

LAURA NYRO

I was maybe 20. I had a now-and-then kind of boyfriend. He was an artist, a real free spirit, and I think I feared him because I found him too truthful. He scared me then in a way that would not scare me now. But he would drift in and out of my life, often appearing at odd hours. Once, late at night, I came back from a fraternity party where I'd gone with another guy and where I had no business being, and I felt as though my spirit were ready to leave my body, as though it were saying, "Well, if THIS is how you want to live, I think I'll just be getting on." I sat glumly on my bed (which was a mattress on the floor, actually very comfortable, and something maybe I should go back to) and I thought, What should I do? I was asking this in the general and the specific way. What I did was to call Dennis, who came and got me and we drove out to the farm where he was living. He made big sculptures there. He wrote poetry. He cooked brown rice. He gardened and went swimming naked in the pond. He kept wildflowers in jelly jars on a wooden kitchen table.

Anyway, we drove out there in his big black pick up truck that had a multitude of problems. It wasn't as much fun as the one time he picked me up on his motorcycle and we went riding in the rain. That night, he rode the thing as though he were dancing with it, dipping the cycle low to one side, then the next. "You're such a great rider," I shouted in his ear, above the noise of the engine.

"It's the LSD," he shouted back.

He came to get me one afternoon and had brought along Laura Nyro's first album. He knew I loved music—those were the days when I had callouses on my fingers of my left hand from playing my guitar. He asked if I had ever heard Laura Nyro, and I said no. He put on an album and we lay down and listened.

After, I had no words I could say to him. I was fuller than full, in the way that music can make you be. Finally I managed, "That was...that was...."

"That was your first acid trip," he said.

That guy moved away, to Tahiti, and it was a few years ago that I heard he'd died of a heart attack. I had to hold really still when I heard that. And I had to listen again to Laura Nyro.

Everyone is always in a hurry these days. Everyone is so distracted. But if you can give yourself a wee island of time, Google Laura Nyro's "Upstairs by a Chinese Lamp," close your eyes and listen.

I miss Laura, too.

THE BOOK OF HOMER

*Until one has loved an animal, a part of one's soul
remains unawakened.*

Anatole France
French poet, journalist and novelist
1844-1924

INTRODUCTION*

*He spoke through tears of fifteen years how his dog and
    him traveled about
The dog up and died, he up and died
After twenty years he still grieves*

-*Mr. Bojangles*, Jerry Jeff Walker

When I first heard that song, I cried out to a friend,
"For twenty years!" I was filled with a combination
of admiration and disbelief. "Twenty years!" I said.
No disbelief surrounding that notion, anymore.
Because I suppose I will grieve that long over
Homer, too. But it's not a hardship. It's not some-
thing I want to be rid of. It's testimony.

This morning, I was walking Gabby, my
other, younger dog, and a little kid came over to
pet her. There was a festival of mutual admiration
that went on for a long time, and finally I tugged
on Gabby's leash and said goodbye to the little
kid who stared mournfully after us as we walked
away. The child's mother reached for her hand.
"That dog's not coming back," she said. "So let's
go."

I had been thinking I'd like to make a little
book of posts about Homer, but I wasn't sure of
the timing. Wait too long, and I'd forget certain
details. Start too early and I'd be too raw; I'd do
more weeping than typing. I guess I've been
waiting for a sign. So, all right, let's go.

---

* In writing about animals, it is standard practice to use the pronoun
"it." No such practice will be followed here.

I am sharing these posts about Homer for a lot of reasons, not least of which is to persuade readers to a certain point of view, which is that there are no bad dogs, there are only bad people who pervert a dog's natural instincts toward boundless joy and affection and loyalty. If you take a chance on a dog who has been abused, you can be rewarded with a love that in my experience is unparalleled.

FINDING HOMER

The first golden retriever I had was a dog named Toby. I picked him out of all the other puppies because he was hogging all the toys and I thought that reflected a kind of tenacity I admired. He turned out not to be a toy-hogger at all, really; he turned out to be a really sweet animal. Did you ever meet a person whose eyes—irrespective of their age—told you they were an old soul? That's what Toby was, an old soul dog. Even people who said that they otherwise did not like dogs, liked Toby. I lost him at seven years old, which is ridiculous, but cancer has no regard for whom it strikes or when, and it likes nothing better than to spring black surprises. I had tried surgery as a last-ditch effort for him, but he died on the table, or more precisely they never let him come up out of anesthesia because what they found guaranteed that there would be no cure and an awful life, should he continue on. So I let him go. And then I went outside and practically howled at the blue sky, and then I fell into a deep depression. The next day, I went out and got another puppy, a sweet little golden girl whom I had decided to call Gracie. She wasn't quite old enough to come home when I picked her out; I would have to wait a couple of weeks.

But I couldn't stand it. I couldn't stand not having a dog around. I like their sounds, I like the way they offer a calm and watchful presence, I like the way their paws smell, I like the way they squeak their squeaky toys and I like the way they walk before me with their tail wagging like a nationalist carrying a flag in a parade and I like the way they raise one paw and their upper lip when they're delicately sniffing something. Most of all, I love the way they love me. There is nothing like a dog's love.

One day I looked at the ads in the paper, just to see....There was an ad for a year-old golden that someone had to get rid of. A year old, huh? I thought, *I can handle a puppy and a year-old golden, and it might be nice to have two dogs.* The old one could teach the puppy things she needed to know. I called the number, and the man who answered told me that he had to get rid of the dog because he and his son just didn't have time for him. He was fine, a great dog; he just didn't have time for him. So I agreed to come and have a look. I went to the bank for cash to buy him, because who did I think I was fooling, saying I'd just have a look?

When I arrived at the address the man had given me, I heard some barking and went around to the back of the house to where the sound was coming from. There were glass patio doors and you could see into the basement, and I saw a small cage in which a rather large golden was housed. He couldn't stand up, he couldn't turn around, but I could see his handsome face and I could see he was trying to wag his tail.

"You here for the dog?" I heard someone say and I turned around to see a man who identified himself as the neighbor who lived behind this house.

"I don't know," I said. "I came to look at him."

"Well, I hope you take him," the man said. "He's in that cage all day long. They only let him out to go to the bathroom, and when they do that they tie him up on a real short rope and he just barks and barks and barks."

I peered in to look at the dog again. Poor guy. I went back to my car to wait, and soon the man who lived there showed up. He invited me into the house and we went into the basement and I saw that actually there were two dogs down there: one was a kind of hunting dog, and he too was housed in a cage that was far too small for him. The man let the golden out and I saw that he was way too thin, and his lower eyelids were drooping like a St. Bernard's. I asked if I could take the dog for a walk and the man shrugged and said sure. I clipped a leash on him and set off down the block. The dog peed an ocean and then pooped and what he pooped let me know he was not healthy.

I took him back to the man. I didn't want a sick dog. But I couldn't bear to leave him there. I thought, I'm going to get him out of here and then I'm going to find him a home. I told the man the dog looked like he had some health problems. The man said nothing. I said I would give him half of the money he had asked for, which was a lot, and no more. The man's face darkened; he was angry.

"This dog is sick," I said.

"Fine," the man said, and took the money. I put "Deeno" which is what the man had named him, in my car, and he immediately jumped out the window to be back with the man who had so abused him. The man got him back in my car, and told me, "Take good care of him."

Right.

The dog jumped all over the car, sniffing for food. When I got him home, he drank a full bowl of water and vacuumed up a full bowl of dog food. I took him to a groomer—he had fleas, and I took him to the vet—he had an ear infection in both ears and was malnourished and he had sores on his neck from his rope tether rubbing on him.

I hated the name Deeno and he didn't know it anyway. Bill and I decided to call him Abner, but he wouldn't come to it. And then one day, a few days after he had been with us, a name suddenly occurred to me. I said it out loud: "Homer?" And he came to me.

It wasn't long after his impromptu christening that he began to reveal some disturbing characteristics, the most awful being that he would suddenly attack. I was putting away laundry one day and I had my back to Homer and he came over and bit me in the behind. It sounds kind of funny, and I guess it might have been, but it mostly just shocked me. A Golden who bit?? Well, yes, unfortunately, a Golden who bit. He bit us and he tried to bite others, including children. He would go on rampages where he ran in circles snapping and growling and if you tried to look into his eyes, there was no contact you could make; he was just gone. I remember once using a pillow to herd him into the bathroom and locking him in there for a few minutes. When he came out he was calm, it was like nothing had happened.

I have had dogs all my life and I think of myself as pretty good with them. But I couldn't work with Homer. Most of the time he was okay, but every now and then he just seemed to lose his mind. "Get rid of him," a friend who also loves dogs advised. "He'll never change."

I tried to calm him down for a few more weeks, and then I gave up and called the Golden Rescue League. They couldn't take him because he bit. Best option was probably euthanasia. I couldn't do it. I gritted my teeth and worked with him some more. And some more. And finally, he started coming around. He didn't have cuckoo fits, he didn't bite us, and although we didn't trust him around strangers for a long, long time, he finally showed us that we could trust him with them, too. Except for the mailman. That poor mailman. Every day when he came, Homer hurled himself against the door as if he had caught sight of his mortal enemy and was going to kill him dead, just as soon as he broke down the door. Every Christmas, I gave that mailman a really big tip, which he totally deserved.

Homer turned into a good dog. He turned into a great dog. Our love for him grew year by year. When he was seven, I got another puppy. Homer wasn't quite sure about this interloper named Gabby at first, but he soon became pals with her. They took walks together. They slept together. They inspected each other's ears. They used to have tug-of-wars when we were trying to watch the news on television, and we'd have to turn the sound way up. My favorite thing was when one casually passed the other by, and he or she would offer a lick, a quick kiss.

It was more work having two dogs, but it was a pleasure, too. They were the little family within our family. And Gracie the cat insinuated herself into the dog family; she was their little sister. And then, at 12 years of age, Homer suddenly got old. And you know what? I was surprised. That dog seemed like he'd be hale and hearty forever. The posts that follow here are a collection of things I wrote about Homer, a kind of scrapbook, ending with his death. They are here to honor him, to remember him, to celebrate the long life of an animal who had a rough start but then a glorious life—even, I suppose, up to the end. But I never wanted there to be an end to Homer. These words keep him with me a little.

HOMER STORIES

Once, when my friend Phyllis' husband, Fabrice, stayed with us, he told Phyllis that Homer kept checking on him in the night. Phyllis said, why didn't you just close the door? Fabrice said, "I liked it, he was like a guardian angel."

Phyllis told me that in an email, and when I read it, I laughed. And then I gave a nice pat on the head to Homer, who said, "What? What are you laughing about?"

A frigid winter day, and Homer needed out. At first I was all, oh the sun is out and the snow is so sparkly, this isn't so bad, I think I'll take him all the way around the block. Then I got in the shade and the wind was a-blowin' and holy moly. I yanked on his leash and said, "Jeez, hurry *up* and *poop!*" He trotted quickly down the driveway toward the door when we got home, I'll tell you.

Last night, in the middle of the night, I woke up and I was really dizzy and the room was tilting. I said out loud, "Something's wrong," and then I went back to sleep. This morning, I woke up and I was still dizzy. I walked Homer and the fresh air made me feel a little better, so I thought, what if it's a leak in the house or something? What if it's carbon monoxide or gas? So I called the gas company and they hooked me up with the para-medic dept. I told them it was *not* an emergency, but here they come a ridin' into town with their sirens going. They checked the house, took my heart rate and blood pressure, and asked if I wanted to go to the hospital. No! I said, but I did kind of want to fix them breakfast. I mean, I have a lot of bacon. So they left, and that was my excitement of the day. Homer had a really good time. Oh, men in uniforms!! he seemed to be saying, as he kept sniffing one guy's crotch, and the guy was all embarrassed and said, "I think he smells my dog."

When I walked Homer tonight, I was considering the fact that I'll very likely develop macular degeneration, given my parents' history, and so I was paying so much attention to what I was seeing: stains from the rain on the sidewalk, the little leaves on the bushes, the big ones on the trees, the light changing in the sky, the sign for Oak Park Little League on the baseball field, Homer's tail wagging to beat the band because he got to go onto the ball field, all the porches I walked past with the lights on in the house and all the gardens. It made me damp-eyed, not with sorrow, but for how rich the world is in all its details. To paraphrase Emily in *Our Town*, how can we ever possibly realize this world? It's just too *much* to think about what just one of our six senses brings us.

I just took Homer for a ride in the car. The whole time, he was in the back seat saying, WOWLOOKATTHATWOWLOOKATTHAT WOWLOOKATTHAT!!!

It is twelve noon on a Sunday. I am still in my pajamas. I read the paper this morning. I made buttermilk pancakes and pepper bacon for breakfast. While I was cleaning up, I noticed Homer sitting in front of the back door, staring intently out. That door, which is mostly glass, is his television. He watches for squirrels in the yard, he watches the birds at the feeder, he monitors the comings and goings of my neighbors. "What are you looking at, pal?" I asked him this morning. He looked quickly over at me, then away; he didn't want to be disturbed. I sat down on the floor beside him and put my arm around him. We sat there for some time, looking out together at the falling snow, the red cardinals, the swift flight of the rabbits who see something that scares them and run away to safety.

When I was in college, I proudly displayed a photo of my boyfriend, whom I thought was the most handsome boy in the world. All the girls would come and swoon over the photo—that is, until he unceremoniously dumped me about ten minutes into the relationship. Would that I had had my priorities straight and displayed the photo of someone who knows what love and loyalty really are. As in:

I give you 13-1/2 year-old Homer, photographed by Teresa Crawford. I hope I look this good when I'm 94.5 years old.

"Did you think he was dying?" Bill asks me this morning, about Homer.

"Yes," I say. "I was afraid of that."

So let's back up a bit.

Yesterday morning, the sun was out after a day of rain. A sunny day in October is an offering nobody should pass up. I decided that I would go to Wisconsin, to Hartford, where I once had a second home. It would be a nice day trip, a chance to look at the leaves, but mostly it would be a chance for Homer to get out of the house and out of his cone of shame, as they call it. He's been wearing it for weeks, because he won't leave his paw alone. The antibiotics are working but not as fast as we'd like, and the healing is not made better by him licking it. Each day we give him a chance, he blows it, and the cone goes on.

But yesterday, I removed the cone with a flourish. Homer was lifted into the car, an indignity he endures for the sake of a ride. Gabby leaped into the car like Superwoman, and I could almost see Homer thinking, "I used to do that too, you know. Only I did it better."

We drove for a while, stopped for lunch and the dogs each got a cheeseburger which they ate with astonishing speed.

We admired the palette of turning leaves, the rolling hills of the Kettle Moraine, and stopped at Pike Lake State Park, where Homer used to go swimming and for long walks. In those days, I would throw a stick out into the lake and Homer would go flying into the water, swim fast, approach the floating stick in a kind of calculating way, then reach his neck out like a snapping turtle, seize the stick and return it to shore. Rinse and repeat.

But yesterday, he was lifted carefully out of the car, both dogs were leashed, and we began walking a trail beside the lake. Eventually, I released Gabby and she ran around in a way that gives new meaning to the term whirling dervish.

"Let Homer off, too," Bill said, and I said, "I'm afraid Gabby might hurt him." Gabby has not yet comprehended that Homer can't play like he used to, and she often jumps on him like the olden days, which knocks him over. But finally I decided, oh, why not, let him be free on this glorious Fall day. We'll make sure Gabby doesn't hurt him. I released him and he started trotting, which he does not often do these days, and then he began nearly running.

Into the lake.

"*No no no no no no no no!*" Bill and I were yelling, but Homer was yelling back, in his dog way, "*Yaaaay, throw the stick, throw the stick!*"

"*Homer!*" we said. "Come!"

He stood in water up to his belly staring at us, confused.

"Come!" we said.

He looked out over the waves. A swim would be so nice, he seemed to be thinking, never mind the fact that the water was freezing. Never mind the fact that he no longer has the strength to swim. If he made it out a few feet, he'd never make it back.

I started thinking, I'm going to have to go and get him. I had it all figured out. I'd bring him in and then I'd sit in the car with the heater on and him in my lap.

But he did come out. He came out and fell down and couldn't get up. For a minute, we all stood around, Gabby, Bill and I trying to figure out what to do. Three beings standing around watching an inert fourth. We might have been a construction crew.

Finally, I snapped the leash on Homer and said, very gently, "Come on, buddy, you can do it." And he did it. He got up, shook himself off, and then came on a quite lovely walk.

Unfortunately, both he and Gabby walked through some stinky water at the side of the path and perfumed the car all the way home.

After the dogs ate dinner and went out for their post prandial walk, I gave them both a shower. Bill and I dried them off and then we watched some political shows that had us practically screaming in outrage. So, you know, a typical night.

I was headed off to bed when I saw that Homer was shaking. "What's up, Home?" I asked him. "Are you cold?"

I thought maybe he hadn't been dried off well enough and so I took warm towels from the dryer and dried him again. Then I put blankets on him. Then I lay on the floor next to him to give him my body heat. Still shaking.

I thought, Is he in shock? Was this day too much for him? In trying to give my dog a beautiful day, did I kill him?

Eventually, he stopped shaking, and I lay on the floor with him for a while longer. At 1:30 I went to bed, and Bill stayed downstairs with Homer.

At 4 a.m., I went downstairs to check on Homer. All was well. Gabby had stayed downstairs too, in a show of support, and she was sound asleep. I saw that Homer seemed okay, but I wanted to be sure, so I got a dog treat to see if he'd eat it. He did, lying on his side like a fat Roman emperor who's eating peeled grapes. Back to bed. Up a few hours later to give a very much alive Homer a little massage and a promise that if he came upstairs he could have his breakfast.

He ate all of his breakfast and part of Gabby's. He went out for a walk. He barked the whole time I ate a bagel because he wanted a bite. Which I finally gave him, which is why he barks all the time when you're eating; I am a terrible teacher of dog table manners.

Today is another sunny day, and it will be a day of rest for valiant Homer.

I did think he might die. (See much earlier story about what a dramatic kid I was. And am.) I was thinking two things. One was, You idiot. You killed your dog. The other was, If he dies, it was on the day that was the best day he's had for a long time. He got to go on a car ride. He ate a cheeseburger. He went back into a lake he loves one more time. He walked along a beautiful trail in the woods and smelled a million smells. He lay by one of the people he loves and got warm.

Right now, Homer's asleep on the landing, halfway between my office and the kitchen. I can feel him feeling me.

People say all the time that they love their dogs. What an understatement.

One of those Fall days mild in temperature, with a pale blue sky and the red and yellow and coral-colored leaves exhorting us to look now, before they're all gone. Thus it is that the dogs and I set out for a walk. We've not gone even two blocks when something happens, an unevenness of pavement, perhaps, or an indentation in the earth, that makes Homer fall. Or not fall, precisely, but tip over. He rises quickly to his feet, I'm glad to say, since I have not brought my cell phone and naturally the first thought that crosses my mind is, oh no, he won't be able to get up and I can't even call a cab to get him home. He is not such an alarmist, old Homer, he is more of a take-it-as-it-comes kind of guy. If you drop something on him or you accidentally step on him, you apologize profusely, and he offers the dog version of "Quite all right. Really."

So anyway, yes, he rises to his feet and keeps on walking. No obvious ill effect except that I am again reminded of his fragility. We walk several blocks and toward the end, he's tired: his head is down, his pace slow, and he's abandoned smelling things.

"Almost home," I tell him, and the tenderness I feel toward him makes me feel stretched inside. I'm thinking, I took out a steak to thaw for dinner, and guess who's getting half? I'm thinking, when we get back, I'll take him into the downstairs TV room with me so I can do laundry and watch the Sunday news shows. He'll collapse on the floor, and I'll put his water dish nearby. And a marrow bone. And the bear toy he likes quite a bit, though he does not squeak it the exuberant way he used to, which was akin to Robert Preston leading the band. I thought, I'll let him rest a few hours, and then I'll make him some dinner.

When we got home, he hesitated before climbing the one step into the house. Oh, man, I thought. He really needs a rest. I might have to carry him downstairs.

However. He came in and stood there.

"Want to go downstairs?" I asked. He always wants to go downstairs. He likes it down there. But today, he stood a while longer and then made the rather laborious trip up the stairs into the kitchen. That place is more strategically located, in case I decide to go upstairs OR down. Which only goes to show you his valor and intelligence and determination to live life as close to the way he used to live it as possible, and it goes to show you my ignorance, which today, I'm happy to have.

A Homer the Wonder Dog Update. Bill and I went to Minnesota for Thanksgiving, and Homer came along. I made him a bed in the back of the SUV with softer-than-soft blankets, and he positioned himself close to us so that he could overhear the good gossip. We stayed in a pet-friendly hotel, and so Homer got to take walks around the place, up and down halls, and ride up and down the elevator. He was out of the cold and the rain getting a bit of exercise, and he wagged his tail to beat the band doing it. We had our friends Jeff and Dan come to the hotel on Wednesday night for take-out Chinese, and Homer lay bedside our table, present as could be, which only made me wonder why all restaurants don't allow dogs. I would pay extra to go to a restaurant that allowed dogs even if I didn't have my dog. If you're a little irritable, watch a dog wag his tail and feel your spirit ascend. If you find yourself unappreciative of the miracle of food, watch a dog lick a plate. Etc, etc.

Anyway, Homer got to come to two dinners, including Thanksgiving, of course. He was admired and pet by many, who peered at him under his cone of shame. He's had to wear that thing for so many weeks now. His paw just won't heal. Today, another vet appointment.

He's begun having some times of restlessness at night. I'm not sure if he's in pain or if the night does not offer the distractions of day, and so he is more aware of that dang cone and of other minor difficulties. Last night, we couldn't ask him to walk up three flights of stairs to go to bed, and Bill slept in the basement with him. This morning, Bill told me that Homer had about an hour of great unease, that he kind of bumped his cone repeatedly against Bill's face. So Bill took the cone off and just pet him and Homer licked and licked and licked his face. "I had a morbid thought," Bill said. "I thought, what if he's dying and he just wanted to say goodbye?"

I admitted that I had those thoughts, too, that there are times I look to make sure he's still breathing. This happens when he has his awfully lethargic times, when I have to persuade him to raise his head to have a drink of water. But then he pops up like a jack-in-the-box for a cookie. Always, Bill and I must remind ourselves that he has the great wisdom of dogs, which lets him know that when he is with those whom he loves and who love him, he is fine at the center of things. Yes, his paw may bother him; yes, his joints may ache; yes, his energy may be low, but he is loved and he feels that the most.

I sat beside him on the floor just now, and looked into his great dark eyes which looked very tired to me, and I worried that it won't be much longer. But the pain is all my own; Homer is only doing what he always does, ever since I first met him, which is to be in the moment without judgement. And with total acceptance.

I'll tell you something a little indelicate. His paw stinks. This despite wound care, despite antibiotics. I could open a door, no matter the cold, to air the place out. I haven't, though. Not quite yet. You know why? Because it's Homer.

Back from the vet. On Wednesday, Homer will have surgery to have that dang toe amputated. "We'll do his anal glands, too," his vet, Dr. Thomas, said. "We can cut his nails. Do you want me to do his teeth, too?"

"Might as well," I said. "Make it spa day."

So we'll see if it's cancer, but mostly we will make it so that Homer will not need dressing change after dressing change and life under a hood. He will have some pain after the surgery, of course, but that will be managed with pain meds. And then I hope he'll be home free for a while. Hope is the thing, isn't it?

I have to tell you, this vet is so good. You would think Homer was his dog, so patient and compassionate is he. It's wonderful if you have a good doctor. But a good vet? Rubies.

For all you Homer the dog fans: He's out of surgery and *fine*. I asked when he could come home, and Dr. Thomas said, "Between three and seven." I said, "I'll be there at 2:59."

May I tell you all how much your comments of support on this page meant to me and Bill? No, I probably can't. But then again, you probably know. Thank you. Thank you. Thank you.

Gabby: Does this mean that now the focus of attention will finally be back on ME? Also, if he isn't hungry when he comes back, can I have his food? I think he really likes chicken. And steak.

Here's a photo of Gabby guarding her best friend, Homer:

And one of her best friend, smiling, because he's almost over the hump:

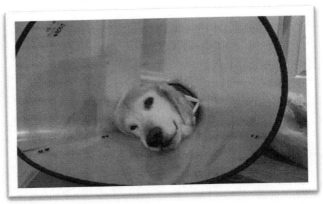

STILL HAPPY | 159

He went out today without our having to assist him, he ate a big breakfast, and now he's going to take a nap. When he wakes up, I'm going to pet him until he says, "Uh, okay, then. That's enough." He has to wear his cone until his dressing is off; then he'll be Free Dog.

Some people don't believe in miracles. I say you just have to keep the scale small. Homer's recovery is miracle enough for me. And, man oh man, am I grateful.

 GABBY

Gabby: I see that someone requested that I weigh in here, amid all the Homer stuff. Amid all the Homer, Homer, Homer, Homer, Homer stuff.

Me: Someone did say they'd like to hear from you. Would you like to say something?

Gabby: Let me sit at your desk chair. I've been practicing my typing.

Me: Okay. *(I stand beside the computer)*

Gabby: *(Looking up at me)* What?

Me: What?

Gabby: Don't watch. Go and make a peanut butter and grape jelly sandwich, like you were just fantasizing.

Me: How do you know I was fantasizing about that?

Gabby: Oh, man. What you don't know about what we dogs know. But run along. Let me talk to the people here.

Me: ....Okay, but don't hurt my computer.

Gabby: Have I EVER hurt your computer?

Me: No. But you've never typed on it.

Gabby: True. But run along anyway.

Me: Okay.

Gabby: Ah. Alone at last.

Hi, everybody. First of all, let me say I'm so honored that someone missed hearing from me, as I have very much missed talking to you.

The most exciting thing going on here is that I get to have hamburger mixed in my kibble lately. I don't know how long it will last, and I don't want to jinx anything, so 'nuff said.

The other exciting thing is that the heat has broken and so I can lie in the back yard and wait for the dogs on the other side of the fence to come out. We have play fights and our owners have heart attacks and yell and call us back but we're just funning. They get so worked up: "GABBY! Come HERE!!! No fighting with those DOGS!!!" Kind of fun.

Also, I have been spending time with my pal, Homer. We lie in the same room and sometimes I give him a little lick when I pass by him. I know my roommates Elizabeth and Bill get very sad about him sometimes, but that is because they forget to be philosophers. Also they forget to be present in the moment, which is something dogs are great at. All those people who write books about being in the moment? Ha. They could help people a lot more by saying one thing: GET A DOG.

We are natural being-in-the-moment-ers. Accidentally step on our tail and what do we do? Yelp, and then wag our tail, because we love you and we have moved on. And so on.

Other news, though not exciting, is that I got groomed the other day. I hate getting groomed. I do not like the hair dryer and I do not like my skirts puffed up like a poodle and I do not like to get sprayed with their dopey perfume and I hate those neckerchiefs. I am more of a classic dresser than that. If I wore clothes, it would be Chanel. If you want to put something around my neck, make it a double strand of pearls. Tahitian.

Whew. This typing has worn me out. I hunt and peck, you know. And speaking of hunting, I'm going out to the back yard where the peonies are blooming and iris are coming up and there is a lot of lavender. I can hardly decide what to pee on. Oh, maybe you don't know. I pee like a boy sometimes. I learned it from Homer. Also I learned — and am learning — courage and fortitude and an immense, immense love that glows in the dark. Homer is the furry Buddha. I am his grateful disciple. I guess everyone in this house is except for the parakeet who never thinks of anything but when he'll get his next fix of cilantro.

Homer news, for his ever-growing number of fans: His biopsy came back for malignant melanoma. That's the bad news. But the good news, the better news, is that there are clean margins after the surgery. So we're kind of back to square one, given his age, which is that we expect to have him for a while yet, in relatively good health, and with a spirit so strong and true, it shines. Look at him: can you see it?

Homer's babysitter fell through, so he's coming to my dental appointment with me. I hope it won't be a problem. If I ran the world, dogs would be allowed everywhere. Especially at the dentist's.

His Homerness. The bandage is so he won't have to wear that stupid cone. Also, it is a red badge of courage.

HOMER REPORT: A+. He had a dressing change today, gets his stitches out on Wednesday. He followed me wherever I went in the house. He played with one of his toys, a plush gingerbread cookie girl. (He wants me to tell you that he also has a football.) He went all the way around the block, trotting like he was a harness racer at the track. He ate all of his breakfast and all of his dinner and barked when I was eating dinner until I shared some of my food. (I know, I know, shouldn't do that, but I had to. That face. That soul.)

Happy snowy December night to the world. I wish you good reading before you sleep and dreams of Golden Retrievers.

Back from having been in California for a few days, and I notice a difference in Homer. Walking slowly. Panting, as though he's out of breath a little bit, even at rest. But comfortable. Smiling, even. That dog always smiles. He is a big dog, a Golden, and I have always loved his size. But right now, I wish he were the size of a kitten, and I would make a sling and carry him around with me every second. I know the inevitable is getting closer. I make him rice. I make him chicken. I pet his head and tell him he is such a good boy. That I love him so much. I give him a biscuit. I ask him if he wants to come downstairs with me while I work on a quilt. He may have less and less energy, but that dog wants to be with you. And boy oh boy, I with him. Earlier today, I leaned against the door jamb, watching him sleep, and wept. But that is no way to celebrate a champion. I ask the force to remind me over and over again that he had—and is having—the best life he could. Still, I want more. Seven more years, at least. 70.

Yesterday was not a great day for Homer. He didn't want me out of his sight. Ate far less enthusiastically, and less than normal. He was preeeetttty low energy. Today he is better, his tail at high mast, his eyes bright and alert and he gobbled up breakfast. This is how it's going to be. Up and down. This morning, Bill asked me to sit beside him. I knew he was trying to figure out the best thing to do for Homer. We said nothing, and then I said, "As long as he's not in pain and he enjoys his walks," and Bill agreed and we were done with our talk. Now we watch and wait and love him up. If his life starts to pin him to the mat, we will help him out.

I saw a nature video this morning that showed a thunderstorm. The sky lit up, the thunder rumbled. Below, a lake stayed placid, the trees did not move, and in the darkness there was great peace. I want to be the lake and the trees for Homer.

You know how when your baby is born, you look into the nursery and you see all those babies and there's only one for you? Oh, you look at the other babies, and they're swell, every one of them can make you smile, but there's only one baby in that nursery for you and that is the baby that is yours. You look at your baby and your heart swells and takes on a certain weight that will never leave.

So it is with dogs, a bit. I have gotten so much consolation from your posts, so much wisdom. You have all helped so much to even out the rough edges. You have shared your stories of your own pain in having to say goodbye to one of your best friends, if not *the* best friend. And I have shared your pain and profited from the care and compassion you have shown me. But I am feeling what I'm sure a lot of you might have felt. I love all dogs. But this one? This is Homer.

Who today had to be persuaded by a slice of roast beef to get up and go outside. But he did it, and he wagged his tail.

Today or tomorrow I get test results for him that will determine the next step. In the meantime, I'm spending a lot of time lying next to him, petting that great head, talking to him. We listen to jazz, too. And he shares his roast beef. When he's sound asleep, I come up to my office to get a few things done, like writing this post. But when he barks for me, I come. Happily.

The biggest feeling I'm having is one of enormous gratitude that I got to rescue a one-year-old from a life of hell, and give him the life he knows now; I got to share 13 years with him. In other news, robins are building a nest on my deck. The flowers I planted yesterday are standing up taller, as though checking out their new digs. Their colors are so bright and cheerful. The sky is so blue, the leaves so green. Tonight I'm making little baby Asian meatloaves and maybe an apple pie. Yin and yang.

When I was a girl, I gave some nuns a spiritual bouquet, which is a promise to say X number of prayers on someone's behalf. I promised some extraordinary number, truly impressive. I would like to say that I honored that promise, but I did not. After I while, I kind of gave up, but figured that at least I'd gotten some brownie points. Or maybe not. Maybe after I made my earnester-than-earnest presentation, the nuns looked at each other and winked.

Even then, I was not entirely convinced of the power of prayer or positive thinking or inordinate determination or whatever you want to call it. I knew lots of great things happened for my mom when she lit candles to ask for this and that, but.....

Many of you have written posts saying you're sending prayers for Homer. And guess what? He's better. I don't know how to account for it, so I'm just going to say that it was you all and I'm going to thank you from the bottom of my doubting heart.

Homer is not leaping tall buildings in a single bound. But he's more alert, he's climbing stairs without his helper sling, his appetite is good. We have enjoyed some good days, and we hope for more, because we are greedy.

I find that one of the hardest things to do when someone you love is ill, animal or person, one of the hardest things to do is to separate yourself from the experience, to realize that if you owe someone compassion and caring, you also owe them the space to have their own journey as distinct from your own. I don't want to fall into despair because Homer is slow, or limping, or not seeing or hearing very well. I want to celebrate his being here, and especially his being here the fine way that he has been for days now.

I'm up in my study, he's downstairs barking because no one is with him right now. So I'll go down and say, "What's up, Bud?" and he'll wag his tail. Some gifts are not wrapped, and this will be one of them.

I am spending time with Homer, who, despite his deteriorating health, perseveres. He can't get up unassisted from a lying down position. He can eat. He is alert. He can walk, though slowly, and with a pronounced limp.

This morning, he was lying on the kitchen floor, whining a little. I lay a folded-up blanket on the floor and then we both lay there, head to head, with me petting him and talking to him, which seemed to calm him down. Together, I think, we listened to bird song and felt the cool breeze coming in from the open kitchen door. I looked at the view from that perspective and it was nice: the underside of the flowers on the kitchen table, the way the walls seemed so much taller. "You know, Homer," I said. "When you go, you are going to be able to run again. And chase balls. And swim in the waters of a big wide lake."

And he said, "If you have to believe that, it's fine. Maybe it's even true. But I am lying beside you now and I am content with my memories and I am glad to hear your human breath going in and out of your body and I am becalmed by the love you are offering me and I am all right, I am all right, I am all right." He licked my hand. I kissed the top of his head. And after a while, I got up to make some pesto pasta because caring for a failing dog is making me hungry all all all the time.

I want to thank all of you who have offered such compassion and wisdom around Homer's decline. I have read every comment and feel such solace. Today Bill sat at the kitchen table reading your comments, looking at your photos, and he too felt the same sense of solidarity with this self-made community. Those of us who love animals in this deep way have offered each other such comfort. I am sorry for all of you (and there are so many of us!) who are dealing with this dilemma yourselves, but I am gratified that we all seem to understand that joy is still very much alive, and all the anguish we might feel is worth it for the companionship we've been given. In a world full of problems and peril, the way we are taking care of each other here is an example of how it could—and should—be done. Thank you.

Here is why it's so hard to decide when to escort a dog out of Dodge. The other day, we were going to call the vet to come over and put Homer down. He couldn't stand without a great deal of assistance, and was just lying so seemingly sad-eyed on the floor all day. "I think it's time," Bill said. And I nodded. But then, "Let's just see if....." I went into the living room and called Homer most emphatically and cheerfully. And that dog got up. He got up and walked into the living room. Since then, he has gotten up every time we need him to: to eat, to go out. Yesterday, he came down some steps and at the bottom, on a tile floor, he slipped and fell, his legs splayed out. He lay still for a while, apparently uninjured, but... bewildered, I would say. Maybe thinking, What is going *on* here? But then, after a while, he got up again.

So. The briefing today will tell you that Homer has been enjoying the front porch, from where he tried magnificently, though thankfully unsuccessfully, to go after the mailwoman.

"Homer!" I said, after I had apologized profusely to her.

"What?" he said.

"Why did you try to bite the mailwoman?"

He looked at me with a little pity in his eyes and then annunciated very clearly, "Because she is a *mail*woman."

So yes, he did that one bad thing, but also he came out back and walked in the yard and regarded the flowers in the garden and sniffed at the clover and then came back up onto the deck where he lay on his side and listened to lawns being mowed, to people laughing in the their back yards, to the drone of airplanes, to the voices of his beloved caretakers talking about how this dog is not ready to go. He is still eating chicken and hamburger and he loves his tiny peanut butter sandwiches which I use to disguise his pills. He likes his massages. He is still wagging his tail. He perseveres and he's not even gritting his teeth, doing it. He does it because this is the next thing, that's all. This is his life now, which he accepts as he has always accepted his life.

Tonight Bill and I went out to dinner. Every time we go out, we have a fear that when we come back.....So tonight we were walking home and Bill said, "I wonder if....." and I said, "I know."

When we got home, I came up to the front door and said, "Well, no yellow head," by which I mean the way Homer used to jump up on the door to greet us. But Bill pointed, and there he was on the floor by the door, so he would know the instant we got back. We came in and greeted him and he was like an old, old grandpa in a wool robe who had waited up for us. Now, seeing that we were home safe, he said, "Okay, then. Good night."

As I write this, the sun is setting and Homer is asleep on the back deck. Soon, he'll come in, slowly but surely, and Bill and I will once again just shake our heads. Homer's 14th birthday is a week away. I'm telling you, he's holding out for the party.

I'm thinking prime rib.

I'm not sure what I expect every morning. I don't expect Homer will be better, not really. But the new day has unwrinkled my heart and mind, as a new day always does, and I come downstairs with a semblance of good cheer.

The situation is that Bill sleeps downstairs with Homer, and I sleep upstairs, as I am with him all day and so Bill takes the nights. So I come down and make coffee and then I go and see how Homer is. Each day, a little more is taken from him, but each day, he seems game to hang on.

This morning, I walked up to him and began to pet him, and Bill told me that in the night Homer had had to go out quickly and he leaped to his feet, and went up the stairs and outside, just like that. I cannot imagine what that cost him. I believe he had a little adrenaline on board that helped him, but still, it must have been hard. What a gentleman. What a champ. He will not go inside.

He didn't seem quite able to do the stairs again, so we carried him up in a blanket/sling, which he seemed not to mind at all and, in fact, might have enjoyed, judging from the look on his face, which was rather like an Egyptian king on his golden litter. We got him to the kitchen door and he went down the deck steps and out, had a proper sniff here and there, then came back in. He's eating less, but he's eating: hamburger, roast beef, eggs, cheese. He's had enough of the peanut butter sandwiches, thank you.

He's sleeping a lot today, peacefully. I wanted to be near him, so I stayed in the kitchen until just now. I had some bananas going bad so I made a banana bread. I made a big salad with bleu cheese and nuts and apples and grapes. I washed and wiped dishes like it was a religious ceremony, which I guess it kind of was because I was watching Homer the whole time and trying to send him messages of peace and calm and love, wordlessly. I read the papers and *The Week*. I tried to work a little on the manuscript for the next book, but I am too taken up to work on a manuscript. That's fine. There will be time later.

I got an email from my publicist sharing a really terrific review that *The Story of Arthur Truluv* got, and I felt funny about feeling happy about it, but I did feel happy about it.

It's three-thirty now, the shadows are beginning to lengthen. Bill has gone to work. Before he left, I said, "Do you want me to call you if anything happens?"

"Of course," he said.

"Because if there's nothing you can do, I don't want you to be at work and all upset," I said.

He said, "No. Call me. I'm in it."

He confessed that he has had his private moments with Homer, down on the floor with him, his own heart stretched and aching. I said, "Yeah, my moments aren't so private." As in this morning after I pet Homer for a long time and then sobbed and sobbed. And Bill put his arms around me and told me that he's old and I said I know, I know, but I still want him, I wish I could still have him, I wish I could just have his beautiful face and wagging tail forever. Gabby came up and licked my face, and Bill consoled me and the irony is that the patient lay peacefully behind us on the floor, breathing in, breathing out, still here and watching us.

You know, that banana bread was awfully good. I'm going to give you the recipe, and I'm going to give it a new name:

HOMER BREAD

1/2 c. softened unsalted butter
1 c. sugar
1 t. vanilla
1 t. lemon juice
2 eggs
3 ripe bananas
1/2 c. sour cream
generous 1/2 t. salt
1 3/4 c. flour
1 t. soda
1 t. baking powder
1/4 c. walnuts, chopped, though I used a few
more
Handful of dates, chopped

Use mixer to blend wet ingredients. Blend dry
ingredients together, then add by spoonfuls to
mixed wet ingredients, running mixer on low.
Add nuts and dates and blend them in quickly.
Bake 1-1/2 hour at 350.

When you cut a slice, before eating it, raise it
up and say, "Here's to Homer and to all good
dogs. And to all good things."

Last night, I spent a long time lying beside Homer. His breathing was shallow but unlabored. I thought it might be time.

This morning, after I helped him up, he walked quite quickly into the back yard, then wanted right back in the house. He refused his pills, no matter how I tried to disguise them. He refused food until I fried him an egg, which he seemed to enjoy quite a bit. No toast, though, unusual for him, who loves bread as much as I do. Just now, he ate some hamburger that had been warmed up. He likes to lie in the breeze coming from the back door, but has no interest in trying to get up again.

It's time.

At 2 p.m., our beloved vet will make a house call and we will help Homer over. I've been trying to be stoic, to understand that it's the right thing to do. Still, "I feel like we're the death squad," I told Bill at the kitchen table this morning as we discussed whether or not we should proceed. "No," he said. "We're the life squad."

I suppose. I know we gave him a good life after the really terrible beginning he had. I know he feels loved and appreciated. I told Bill, "The only way I can do this is to think that I'm doing it for him."

"You are," Bill said.

But oh, how I will miss him. I miss him already. Which is why I'm going back downstairs to lie beside him and talk about various things he loves (Culvers, swimming, Gabby, balls) and pet him until it's time.

Last night, at two in the morning, I read your posts to feel better. I am so very grateful for all your stories and words.

A hard night tonight, and a hard morning tomorrow, I'm sure. And then, gradually, it won't hurt quite so much. But always inside, a big, big place for Homer.

THIS JUST IN: A STAY OF EXECUTION! I hope you will both forgive me and celebrate with me: Homer is among us still. This afternoon, he rallied. He got up with a little assistance, came outside to do his business, and later, when Bill and I were sitting on the deck, got up again by himself to come out and join us. Nearly ordered himself a whiskey sour.

You who have posted here have been with me in mind and spirit. I know that I have reminded you of painful memories of your own and I regret that, except for the fact that I think a wondrous kind of caring and balm have emerged here that has benefited us all. Your stories!

I have no illusion that Homer is "cured," but the vet said if he won't take his medicine (which he still won't, but he is eating) to give it to him with baby food. And let's hold off on plan A. So after having spent the morning crying my heart out, really wailing at times, I am now off to the grocery store for pureed beef stew.

I really am sorry, and I need to ask you: do you need a break from hearing about Homer, or do you want to stay tuned?

At least you got a good banana bread recipe.

Yesterday, Homer walked out in the back yard and did his business, then stood for a while, as though contemplating what it is he wanted to do next. He lay down next to a patch of lavender and I sat beside him for some time. We watched a bee busy himself in the blossoms. Three times, a robin landed on the wire above us with nesting materials in its mouth. It was going to make a place from which to bring forth new life. That is what I'm going to try to mostly think of today.

I believe that those of you who say "It's time now" are advocating on behalf of my dog, and I love you for that. But please understand that the facts are these: he does not appear to be in pain, and in fact I got his (preventive) pain pill down him just now with baby food, as the vet suggested. Homer is amazingly alert. He is still eating—though unpredictably—and doing his business in the back yard. He sleeps through the night, though neither Bill nor I do because we wake up and check on him. He was just now walking around the back yard wagging his tail. This afternoon, he gave Bill's face such a licking Bill won't have to wash for five years.

I am trying the very best I can to pay attention to what I think my dog wants me to do, as is Bill. As is our vet. I do not want to make my dog suffer so that I won't miss him. I do not want him to suffer at all. If and when it comes to that, I will euthanize him. As you know, I was all set to do that today because I thought the big slide was in progress. But all signs seem to point toward it not quite being time yet.

When you're this close to the end, one or two more days feels like much longer. It feels like you've won the lottery. So I'm trying to enjoy the fact of his dear face and his company for the little time I have left. So many of you have said, "You'll know when it's time; there won't be any doubt." My daughter said she knew when it was time with her dog because of his eyes, she said, "He wasn't there anymore." Homer is still here, and I am here for him for as long as it takes.

Homer being guarded by the intrepid Gabby.

I am just up in my study from folding clothes at the kitchen table. We (Homer and I) were hearing Mozart from the CD I have on. He slept well, he ate a little breakfast and took all his pills. He's napping now. I'm ever a nurse; there's nothing I like more than making my patients comfortable.

Early this morning, I took Gabby to the woods for a run off-leash. She didn't run all that much and at one point when I was urging her on, she came to a dead halt and looked at me as though she were saying, "Listen, sister, I'm not as young as I used to be either!" But oh, when she ran flat out, what a sight. And the sound of the birds, there's the real music. It'll be a nice day outside today. And I get to create the weather inside, and I'm predicting joy and appreciation with an occasional, brief shower.

Last evening, at that time of day when it seems like dusk is a hammock for your mind, I took Gabs for a walk in the neighborhood and I will admit that I was hurting bad about Homer. There is a homemade swing on my route hanging low from a big, big tree. It's beautiful but I never see anyone in it. But last night, there was a little boy in it, maybe two or three years old, and his Dad was pushing him and he was laughing that little boy laugh, really loud. It made me unaccountably glad.

If you don't think life is the Giant Mix, you don't know nothing.

HOMER
JUNE 10, 2003 - JUNE 10, 2017
CHAMPION

At five a.m., he awakened us, barking. He'd had trouble walking the night before, and needed to be carried down the steps, but now he wanted to go out. I put his helper sling on and he rose up and walked rapidly into the back yard, where he did his business, then stood there panting, seemingly not quite sure of what to do. We got him back into the house and he refused everything but water. I knew I'd never get his meds into him. In his eyes was a weariness I hadn't seen before, and I remember so many of you saying, "You'll see it in his eyes when it's time." I called our vet, who said he would arrive in about two hours.

Homer rose on his own and wanted out again, and we lay on the back deck for a while. The sky was a beautiful rose color and the sound of birdsong filled the air. There are robins building a nest nearby, and oftentimes they pause on the wire to have a little look-see. Today there were two robins who landed on the wire. They stayed for an uncommonly long time this morning, just looking down.

I pet Homer, I told him he was such a good dog, I told him I had called the vet to help him leave this life so that he would not suffer. I asked if he wouldn't mind, once he was on the other side, sending me a sign to let me know he was all right.

After a while, he wanted up again, and struggled to his feet. I helped him to the steps, but he couldn't seem to muster the strength to go down them. And so I carried him. He found a nice spot by the garden and lay down there. And it is there, with a close up view of clover and grass and flowers that we waited.

He was panting, and when I put my hand to his chest I could feel that his heart had a wild rhythm. I knew it was time, it was best, but I also felt as though I had lain us down on the tracks when a freight train was coming.

When the vet came and administered the sedative, Homer took exception to it and tried to bite him. Then he lay quietly, and I spoke to him and spoke to him.

The vet needed to plug something in, so we moved Homer back up onto the deck. He was breathing easily now, he was very relaxed. I talked to him some more, pressed my forehead into his. And then that was it. I said to the vet, "I think he's gone." The vet listened with his stethoscope and said, "He's at peace now."

He loaded Homer into his car and I gave my beautiful dog one last kiss and stroked his silky ear. I said to the vet, "I hope it was the right time," and the vet said it was. Then he said, "You were lucky to have him. He had great heart."

Boy, do I know that.

Oh, Homer. Happy birthday.

I feel such horrible pain I can hardly breathe, but I also feel glad that he is free, that we did all we could, and he did all he could because we all loved each other so. That dog squeezed everything he could from life up until his last day, and in so doing goes on to serve as inspiration to me.

To all of you who have been on this journey with me, thank you so much for helping me. I'm going to finish weeping and then I'm going to take Gabby for a long walk.

Oh. After the vet left, I lifted a blanket and found fur that the vet had shaved off Homer's leg so that he could start an IV. It is beautiful, golden fur. Homer really was golden. I gathered it up and I will keep it forever. Also, I take it as his first sign.

Yesterday, I got a condolence card from my wonderful vet, Dr. Thomas, about Homer. I cannot tell you what it meant to read "We will never forget him" at the end of his message. Naturally, this reopened a barely healed wound, but in a good way.

Sometimes people have a hard time understanding how much an animal can mean to someone. I think of the white rat I heard about who was cremated, and I thought, wow, I never heard of that. But people love all kinds of animals and it does nothing but good for us to open our hearts to love, whether it's for a ferret or a turtle or a dog or a cat or—the biggest challenge of all—for each other.

Some of you have asked about how Gabby (my other, six-year-old Golden mix) is doing. I would say that mostly what the absence of Homer has done, is to have gotten her to come out of a kind of shyness she had, and onto center stage. This is a big reason I'm hesitant to get another dog, though the sun never sets without my having looked at dogs—old dogs, puppies, all kinds of dogs. Maybe I should start looking at white rats.

This morning I was on the porch with coffee, and a cardinal landed on top of the weeping cherry in the front yard. He delivered a little speech and then flew up on to the roof.

"There's your bird," Bill said, referring to the cardinal I found injured and tried to save.

Maybe it was. Probably it wasn't. The place for the gone is in a pocket of our hearts, or in a little lit place in our brains, or both, thus ensuring that they are not gone at all.

It got hot today, Homer. You wouldn't have liked it. You would have found it harder to walk than usual, you would have panted more. I was thinking about that when I walked Gabby just now, trying to come with reasons why, really, it's good that you're no longer here. But then I thought about how I could have made a neckerchief for you and put it in the freezer for a while before we left, and you could have worn it on the walk. And when you came, in, I could have given you a little ice cube rub down, which I did another time when you got hot and you seemed to really like it.

When I ate dinner, I felt so guilty. I thought it was wrong of me to eat when you can eat no more. I know that's bad thinking, faulty thinking, overly dramatic thinking, but it's what I thought.

I took a long walk with Gabby just now and I thought maybe you were sending me signs that you were around. There was a white baby bootie on the sidewalk, and it looked like one of the nonslip socks I had you wear sometimes toward the end. There was a sign for Invisible Fence that had a Golden Retriever who looked like you, and he was happy and young and strong.

I told a friend today that I wished there really was a rainbow bridge that you crossed and you were happy and playing. But I added that, knowing you, you would stop playing in order to check on us below, those whom you loved so well. I told her I saw you looking down, one ear over your eye in the way it always used to fall, which always made you look coy.

I will miss you forever and that's a fact. Whatever is left of my life, part of it will be always missing you. I guess I wouldn't have it any other way.

You prepared us all. You lost abilities in such a slow-motion way, I could hardly tell how things happened. All of sudden Gabby needed to be walked separately from you because you couldn't keep up. So she got used to walking alone.

Gradually, you stopped crowding me while I fixed your food, and racing to the bowl, then you began eating a little less, then less, so that on the last day when you refused food altogether it wasn't such a shock. You had a little trouble getting up from a lying down position, then more trouble, then a lot of trouble. We got used to everything, so it didn't hurt as much as if it were sudden. You were ever the gentleman, Homer. Yet for all your preparations, there is a sorrowful wind blowing through us all.

On the week anniversary of Homer's death, a friend texts to ask if I want to go with her to see *Wonder Woman.* Yes, I say, though I don't really want to see it. But, you know, diversion from sitting on the front porch and crying.

While trying to watch the movie, I remembered something. Many years ago, I went to a movie after I had been diagnosed with cancer, and at the time the prognosis was uncertain. I went to see a show to take my mind off things, but it proved to be a disaster, because rather than taking my mind off my situation, it amplified it. For me, anything sorrowful that I need to work through is a jealous thing. It wants my attention all the time. That's the only way I'm going to get through something, is to stay in it and keep on moving forward, no matter how hard that may be.

When my friend and I walked back to her car after the movie, we talked about the film a little. Neither of us had really liked it, but we both liked the redemptive end.

After we got in the car, the conversation turned to Homer, and I confessed that I was doing a lot of second-guessing about having put him down, which was utterly useless. I told her that I thought, too late, that maybe, despite his woes, he was willing and wanting to stay longer. What Homer always wanted was to be with us. Even when the stairs were difficult for him, he labored up them to be wherever I was. I would tell him sometimes, "Stay there, okay? I'll be right back." But if I were anywhere more than a minute or two, he would come and find me. In my office, he eschewed his comfortable orthopedic bed up against the wall in order to lie right behind my desk chair. Close. If I were in the kitchen, he lay on the rug right next to me as I was cooking. If I were doing laundry, there he would be, chin on his paws, watching and waiting. His mission was to keep an eye on me, because he liked being with me, but mostly because he was always protecting me—at first ferociously, then with a little more discernment.

Toward the end, when it was so hard to get him up to go outside, I once rang the front doorbell to see if that would jolt him into action. He was up immediately, going to see who was trying to get into his place and possible threaten his people. Never mind that the minute whoever was at the door came in, Homer was all wagging tail and friendliness. Until I told him it was okay, he was ready to kick someone's ass. Even at 14. Even when he couldn't jump up on the door anymore. Even when he walked with a pro-nounced limp and couldn't see much and could hear even less. When the bell rang, he put on his uniform and charged. And so that was how we got him outside that day. A ghost rang the doorbell, and he decided that as long as he was up, he'd pee.

But that was my terrible guilty fear, I told my friend, that I had made a decision that Homer would not have made, and he paid the price. I sat there bawling, saying, "Maybe he thought if the end was going to be tough, then the end was going to be tough, but he was game, that dog was always game. Maybe a few more hours, maybe even a few more days, would have been mostly precious to all of us."

(Here I thought about how after it got hard to get him to eat, what a triumph it was when he ate half of a toasted cheese sandwich I made him! What joy in seeing him take if off the little flowered saucer on which I offered it.)

"Maybe I did the right thing," I told my friend, "but maybe I made a mistake. I keep thinking, what happened after he had that second shot, the one that stopped his heart? He was still alive for a little bit after that, right? I remember I asked the vet if he could hear and the vet said maybe a little. So he was alive for that little bit of time and he was looking right at me, he was looking right at me all that morning, and I am so worried that even though he was hurting at that moment, he didn't want to go." My friend began to cry, and told me about when she put her Golden down. She said, I held onto that dead dog and just bawled. The vet probably thought I was crazy."

I said, "I think the vet sees this kind of stuff all the time, and that all he thought was there's another good person who loved another good animal."

Well, I can second guess myself to death, I guess. But the truth is that in a situation like this, there are no good answers. You pick one, and regret not having picked the other.

I haven't seen any more signs. I haven't heard him barking, I haven't seen glimpses of him, as some have said I would. But he walks with me. And he is enfolded in the mystery and the majesty, whether I see signs or not.

When my friend and I were sitting in the stifling car (and it was funny that neither of us made a move to open a window, as though the heat were the right thing, the intensity, even the uncomfortableness), my friend said, "You know, they are entrusted to us, and it falls to us to decide for them what has to be done. You did what you did out of love. I think he knew how much you loved him." What hurts so bad, even as I type this, is the knowledge that he loved me so much.

I romanticize things, I know. I want to think that he could have had a good bite of prime rib and a deep drink of cool water and died in my arms, staring up at me, obviously at peace. He did not look peaceful before the vet arrived. He looked worn out. I don't think there was ever going to be much on the menu for him anymore. But to give the go-ahead to something that would separate him and me forever, oh, that was hard. It was too irrevocable.

There is one thing that sustains me in all this, a thought I return to again and again. And that is that I could not have possibly done more than I did to give that dog a good and loving home, especially after the hell he endured before I got him.

After he was renamed Homer, we got a post-card from a friend that said he really liked the name, as it befitted both a hero and an idiot. The postcard was kind of funny, but Homer was no idiot.

I named him Homer because it was the name he instantly came to. And because the root of that word (which was what I often called him) is what I always wanted us to be to each other: Home. And we were. Then, now, and always.

Jeez. Today my *parakeet* died. It's never a good time to lose a pet you loved, but this was way too close to Homer.

This bird had belonged to my mother, and I had him for two-and-a-half years. Parakeets are such cheerful little birds, and I enjoyed him. Bill used to bring him downstairs with us when we watched TV, because "he's part of the family." He liked parsley and carrots and millet seed and the CD of birds songs I used to play for him. He loved his mirror, and in fact the day before he died, kissed himself in the mirror.

All my life, people have told me I need to toughen up. All my life, I have not exactly been able to do that. And so I wept quite a bit when Fritzi died. Then I said to Bill, "Let's just move someplace rural and get a whole bunch of animals." He didn't say no, so I take that as a firm yes.

I went out onto the front porch with Gabby. It's a cool summer morning, and I had on a little jacket. I had the paper with me, but I didn't read it. Instead, I listened to the wild birds, and watched them come for berries on the juneberry tree. I watched people walking their dogs. They would be far away, then they would be right in front of my house and Gabby would bark and I would explain to her that that dog was a good dog and so was she, and she would say, oh yeah, I forgot, and stop barking. And then the people would be far away again. And so on.

As an astute person once said to me, "Life. Idn't it?"

I love the idea that if a cardinal pays you a visit,
it's the spirit of someone you loved who has died.
We've had a young cardinal hanging around, and
he's become like a pet. The other day we came
home and were walking up the driveway and he
whistled at us, which I take to be the bird equivalent of a wagging tail. When we come out on
the porch, he flies on over as if he's set to deliver
a casserole for the potluck. He sits on top of the
bushes and looks at us.

"Is that Homer?" I whispered to Bill the other
day, and Bill did not say no.

I love seeing that bird so much I gasp and act
like I'm witnessing a miracle every time he shows
up. Well, I *am* witnessing a miracle: look at the
beauty of that red and black, look at the architec-
ture of the feathers, look at the fact that birds
have internal compasses that make our GPSs look
as sophisticated as pick-up sticks. Here, let me
save you a Google:

"Scientists have thought for years that
migratory birds may use an internal compass to
navigate between their nesting areas and wintering
grounds, which can be separated by thousands of
miles. ... The finding strongly supports the
hypothesis that migratory birds use their visual
system to navigate using the magnetic field."

I put out some birdseed on a paper plate the
other day, hoping he'd come and help himself.

Guess what:

CODA

It's been two months since Homer died. Every now and then, Bill or I have a bad, tearful day, one of those sad and frustrating times of understanding that that our boy really is gone forever. It's a dull ache, how much we miss him, but that ache is beginning to lessen and make room for more joy, more ease. We are not sure we'll get another dog, but we'll see. In the meantime, Gabby has come into her own as the only child. She's more active and responsive. Today, on our walk, we passed a pretty good-looking little poodle, and Gabby made these incredible noises—almost word-like. In fact, the woman with the poodle said, "Does that dog *tallk?*"

"Why yes," I said. "She does." And I was thinking, this is what she's saying: "I'm here! I'm here! I'm here."

So she is.

51965727R00113

Made in the USA
Middletown, DE
15 November 2017